Sales Rewards and Incentives

John G. Fisher

- Fast-track route to recognizing sales performance excellence and keeping sales people motivated and incentivized
- Covers the key areas of financial and non-financial rewards and recognition for sales people, from learning what works and constructing schemes to managing the communication and monitoring results
- Examples and lessons from around the world and market sectors including financial services, IT, automotive and retail
- Includes a glossary of key concepts and a comprehensive resources guide

>>EXPRESSEXEC.COM<<
essential management thinking at your fingertips

SALES
12.07

First Published 2003 by
Capstone Publishing Limited (a Wiley company)
8 Newtec Place
Magdalen Road
Oxford OX4 1RE
United Kingdom
http://www.capstoneideas.com

CIP catalogue records for this book are available from the British Library and the US Library of Congress

ISBN 1-84112-460-5

Contents

Introduction to ExpressExec

ExpressExec is a completely up-to-date resource of current business practice, accessible in a number of ways - anytime, anyplace, anywhere. ExpressExec combines best practice cases, key ideas, action points, glossaries, further reading, and resources.

Each module contains 10 individual titles that cover all the key aspects of global business practice. Written by leading experts in their field, the knowledge imparted provides executives with the tools and skills to increase their personal and business effectiveness, benefiting both employee and employer.

ExpressExec is available in a number of formats:

- **Print** - 120 titles available through retailers or printed on demand using any combination of the 1200 chapters available.
- **E-Books** - e-books can be individually downloaded from ExpressExec.com or online retailers onto PCs, handheld computers, and e-readers.
- **Online** - http://www.expressexec.wiley.com/ provides fully searchable access to the complete ExpressExec resource via the Internet - a cost-effective online tool to increase business expertise across a whole organization.

» **ExpressExec Performance Support Solution (EEPSS)** - a software solution that integrates ExpressExec content with interactive tools to provide organizations with a complete internal management development solution.
» **ExpressExec Rights and Syndication** - ExpressExec content can be licensed for translation or display within intranets or on Internet sites.

To find out more visit www.ExpressExec.com or contact elound@wiley-capstone.co.uk.

12.07.01

Introduction to Sales Rewards and Incentives

» Sales reward options
» Instant incentives

"Most people exert only 15% of their combined intelligence, skills and aptitudes in their employment."

William James, 19th century American psychologist

For a business to be successful, someone somewhere has to sell something. And it has to be done on a regular basis. Other people's jobs and your organization's market share depend on sellers being able to find buyers. But it has never been easy. Nor is it a particularly comfortable profession, especially in a highly competitive world where you are only ever as good as your last sale. Once a seller has hit the target or achieved a goal there is always a tendency to relax or retreat back into clerical tasks. When you stop selling you are not just standing still, you're going backwards because the competition will be out there taking your customers. For that reason the task of sales management in the twenty-first century has to include creating sales rewards and incentive schemes to maintain sales activity after the comfort level has been reached.

SALES REWARD OPTIONS

So, you need to provide something over and above a monthly paycheck to get the best out of salespeople. For long-term motivation it could be a bonus, a commission on every sale or involvement in an annual profit-share program. Tactical, non-cash incentives may include merchandise, travel, store vouchers, the occasional bottle of wine or tickets to the big game. You may even have been tempted to devise recognition schemes to congratulate those who do well. You may have put up wall charts so sellers can see where they are in relation to their colleagues. But do any of these ideas work and if so, what would be the right combination and how much should a sales manager be spending on these extra items?

When you consider that non-cash incentives and benefits can often add up to more than 30% of the average seller's remuneration, it makes sense to devise a package that is both cost-effective and motivational.

INSTANT INCENTIVES

Managing sales incentives has a history of less than 70 years. Formal sales incentive programs were originally devised in the US to stimulate rapid distribution of consumer goods such as cars and financial products.

The detail of such schemes was kept confidential and there was little open debate about what each organization did to improve its sales performance. But now the Internet is with us, very little regarding staff remuneration remains unknown. What you do not know from interviewing prospective sellers you can get from industry surveys and niche Websites. This transparency has led to a problem. If everyone in your sector is being paid the same and has similar benefits of employment, how can you attract and retain new sellers? The answer may well be in the additional rewards, incentives and recognition package.

One growing trend to consider, though, is the fact that more professional sellers are now opting to work from home rather than from an office. By nature they may be more entrepreneurial than the average person but they still need to feel part of a team and need to be communicated with on a regular basis. Managing the process of maintaining contact with your key sellers could be greatly strengthened by introducing incentive programs for all kinds of business activity from better record-keeping to positive involvement in the local community. One thing is certain. You cannot rely on them coming into the office any more. As a sales manager it will be your job to keep in contact with them using interesting and stimulating methods (see Chapter 7).

A second important development is the progress that has been made in tracking sales performance. In the good old days, the sales cycle was usually quarterly or monthly with bonuses being paid at the end of the sales year. Now with almost daily sales tracking in most industries through e-mails and Websites, incentives and rewards can be equally instant. Even travelling around the sales territory can now be monitored in real-time through GPS (global positioning satellite) so you can even know where your sellers have been that day without having to wait for a field report (see Chapter 4, The E-Dimension to Sales Rewards and Incentives).

The combination of incentives, rewards and recognition devices is endless. New ways to reward sellers for achieving excellence are being introduced as instant tracking and communication technology become commercially available. Knowing how to press the right incentive switches and reward levers for your sales team may well be the most crucial skill for sales managers of the future wishing to increase productivity and create effective motivation.

12.07.02

What are Sales Rewards and Incentives?

- Cash schemes
- Non-cash incentives
- Key learning points

Hold-up man: Quit stalling – I said your money or your life.
Jack Benny: I'm thinking it over. . .

Jack Benny

What you should pay your salespeople is always related to what they can sell. The product margins define what can be afforded per sale. You know what an average seller could sell in a year so you can easily set a basic salary. But not everyone is average. You would want to encourage higher sales from those who can produce them, so you need an incremental reward. It could be commission-only but such systems tend only to work for low value/one-sale items. Good commission-only sellers are both hard to find, difficult to keep and may not be totally focused on good customer care.

For most professional sales organizations the debate is largely about what incremental benefits you can offer salespeople over and above a basic salary because successful people will work harder for recognition and non-cash benefits once they have gone beyond their financial comfort zone. Going beyond perks, you may then consider structured incentive schemes with rewards related to sales that could be both cash and non-cash. But the additional cost could be as much as 50% or more of the basic salary. So getting the balance right is vital to keep selling at a profit. Predicting how many will achieve how much, is an art in itself, and programs which actually pay for themselves out of incremental sales are possible, but you need to be able to monitor costs and results carefully.

CASH SCHEMES

Assuming you are paying the going rate for the type of seller you employ, the first enhancement you could consider is a cash bonus. If they are working to an overall sales goal as a team they may share the bonus equally. However this model has disadvantages, as not everyone in the team will have contributed to the same degree either by virtue of their experience or their general level of activity. A number of adjustments may have to be made to make the scheme equitable. For example, you may pay an extra amount for every year of service or for a higher level of technical competence. Another approach could be to divide the total bonus amount in proportion to individual sales made.

Or you could even pay salespeople according to their performance ranking in the sales team. But you will also need to consider what to do about people who leave or join the sales team while the scheme is in progress. You may have to deal with "split sales" where the order is confirmed by the combined efforts of more than one person but not the whole group.

The more equitable you make the scheme, the more rules you will need to cope with anomalies. You will also need to be very clear about what constitutes a sale as industries vary in how they record confirmed sales and take a different view when it comes to renewing an existing contract rather than achieving a genuine conquest sale.

Once you get into the detail of sales team remuneration, it becomes quickly apparent that they cannot be remunerated by salary alone in the same way as operational or administrative staff. There may be a team bonus element as described above but team rewards are often subject to "social loafing" in which individual effort falls when only the group performance is being monitored. This psychological phenomenon was first recorded by a French agricultural engineer, Ringelmann, in 1913, when he instructed his students to pull on a rope attached to a dynamometer. Working alone each student could pull a weight of around 85 kilograms (191 pounds). Together as a group of seven they could only pull 450 kilograms (1012 pounds or 145 pounds each). This represented a fall of around 25% in overall efficiency. The findings remained true over a long series of tests.

Typical cash schemes have therefore evolved to reward individual effort from salespeople. Let's consider how you might tackle adding individual bonuses for personal performance in a sales environment. Firstly you need to create a career path based on salary. Good salespeople are expensive to recruit and train. You need to retain them for as long as they are successful. To encourage career salespeople to progress within the sales organization you will need to have a series of salary upgrades based on experience and number of salespeople supervised. A seller could apply to become a trainee manager after say two years, a full manager a year later and perhaps a regional manager within five years. Often such models will include the need to recruit people for the team and retain those who are already there. The higher up you go, the more quality and administrative targets will need to be included as the nature of the job changes.

The next step could be to set an expected sales threshold for each grade. In general this should be achievable by about 50% of the group and the aggregate contribution to overheads should cover the basic costs of everyone's employment. Beyond the threshold, you could then introduce incremental payments for every sale made, in other words a commission or bonus payment. For the highest flyers you could add an additional bonus for achieving a specific target or for being one of the top ranked performers during the year. Managers could receive a bonus based on the total sales of the team they manage, adjusted according to volume. You will need to make sound estimates of the number of people likely to attain the various levels of achievement before announcing the structure. In overall terms your scheme could provide the opportunity to reward individuals at a rate equivalent to between 0% and 50% of their salary for their individual effort. You need to decide whether the cash scheme should be capped or open-ended, depending on how good you are at predicting performance levels.

In this way you can construct a cash scheme that encourages newcomers to take up a new career, existing sellers to improve their earnings and/or move into management, and top achievers with no management ambitions to write their own paycheck, within reason.

NON-CASH INCENTIVES

But most people, including salespeople, do not work just for the money. Maslow, arguably the most important thinker about individual motivation, sketched out the theory of a "hierarchy of needs"[1] in which human beings progress from the need for basic shelter and security to the need to belong to a group, to the need to be recognized for having a particular skill or contribution and eventually to the need to self-actualize (become the best *you* can be, to be at peace with yourself). (See Fig. 2.1.)

Within a sales organization this suggests that to motivate people effectively you have to satisfy each lower level need before moving on to the next one. There is no point in offering unlimited first class international air travel to someone who cannot keep up the mortgage payments on his or her house. The need for basic security and shelter

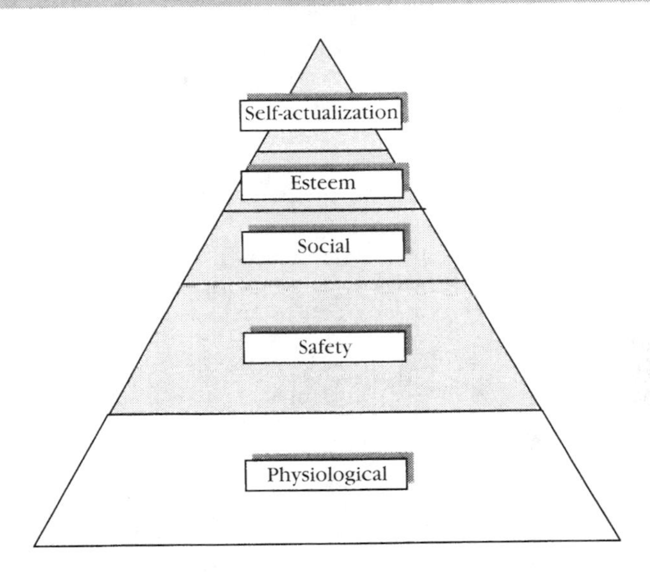

Fig. 2.1 Maslow's hierarchy of needs.

is met with a competitive salary. For any incentive scheme to work effectively, once this need has been met, the next step is to include elements which reinforce belonging, in other words being part of the sales team or organization, through a loyalty bonus, regular meetings or social events. The next need is to be recognized for having a skill. In sales terms this means public plaudits for achieving targets, receiving a phone call of congratulation from the boss or being enrolled in an honors club. At the highest level career salespeople can be motivated by involvement in management decisions, invitations to exclusive company events and support with skills enhancement and professional training. Such "soft" incentives are often supplemented by graded non-cash rewards.

In practice the reward elements of non-cash schemes could include store vouchers, electronic points cards, merchandise, tickets to sports events, individual travel, invitations with partners to conventions and meetings in luxury venues. It may sound frivolous to include such items as elements in a remuneration plan, but it is big business. US companies have spent over $4 billion a year in recent years on so-called "performance improvement programs" and Europe is catching up fast. Last year UK industry sources indicated expenditure of some £2 billion, taken as a whole. But does it work? There are no overall statistics on effectiveness. Every organization and situation is different but within this book there are dozens of examples of successful sales incentive schemes including AEG, Volvo Cars, Mazda, British Telecom, Philips Electronics, and Barclays Bank. Results vary from an increase in sales of less than 10%, to well over 40% using properly structured programs.

KEY LEARNING POINTS

- Sales remuneration is a complex issue and there is always more than one solution. However, the nature of successful selling is such that salary alone will never be enough. You have to provide an element of incentive to encourage regular and positive activity.
- Beyond the "comfort zone," you get diminishing returns from offering more money. As living standards rise and fewer and fewer people operate at subsistence levels, you need to provide a mix of cash and non-cash to tap into the latent capacity of everyone to perform better at their job.
- Non-cash rewards linked to performance are a growing proportion of sales force remuneration.
- Sales increases can be as much as 40% better with a structured, tailored, non-cash performance improvement program.

NOTES

1 Maslow, A. (1954, 1987) *Motivation and Personality*, Harper & Row, New York.

12.07.03

The Evolution of Sales Rewards and Incentives

- Rewards and incentive theory
- Applying the theory
- Practical examples
- Holistic approach
- Key learning points

> "In order to meet the competitive role requirement, a person should be favorably disposed toward engaging in competition. Managers should also enjoy rivalry of this kind and be motivated to seek it whenever possible. If they are unwilling to fight for position, status, advancement, and their ideas, they are unlikely to succeed."
>
> *John B. Miner, professor of human resources, the State University of New York*

Rewards and incentives within a business context are nothing more than the commercial management of motivation. Human motivation has always been with us, even though a framework for measuring it has only been considered in a systematic way over the last 100 years. Freud, in the early 1900s, was the first social scientist to discover a direct link between the unconscious, and human thoughts and actions, and stressed the significance of aggressive drives in human behavior. The idea that humans are mainly motivated by the pursuit of pleasure and the avoidance of pain, (the pleasure principle), was first expounded scientifically by the Freud Group. It is comforting to see how this principle could so easily act as a guide for modern managers attempting to motivate unwilling employees. Some experimental psychiatrists broke away from Freud's group in 1912 under the leadership of Carl Jung and began to chart typical personality types, such as extroverts and introverts, as a way of explaining and even predicting social behavior. However, much of this early work was based on relatively few case histories and so some of the concepts were of questionable predictive value.

It was not until the 1930s that serious attempts were made to classify some of the earlier findings. In 1938 Henry Murray set out to categorize human motivation/drive into 20 basic human needs. One of them was the need to achieve:

> "To accomplish something difficult: to master, to manipulate or organize physical objects, human beings or ideas; to do this as rapidly and independently as possible; to overcome obstacles and attain a high standard; to excel one's self; to rival and surpass others; to increase self-regard by the successful exercise of talent."[1]

At about the same time Abraham Maslow (see Chapter 2) was beginning to formulate a theory of human motivation based on a hierarchy of needs that could be predicted (and therefore be useful). Maslow's findings culminated in an all-embracing theory of human motivation that was published for the first time in the *Psychological Review* in 1943. By the 1950s academics were turning their attention toward "actualization", in other words the psychological striving for growth and fulfillment latent in every human being, given the right conditions. This would later become highly relevant for sales managers and their teams. Frederick Herzberg in 1959 introduced the notion of "hygiene factors" to motivation theory, suggesting that there were "satisfiers" and "dissatisfiers" with most occupations and suggesting it was the job of management to increase the former without increasing the latter, to maintain positive motivation. By the 1960s, following the post-war consumer boom on both sides of the Atlantic, some concepts were being used for the first time by commercial organizations to create business policy in the pursuit of more customers. Cognitive dissonance theory, where humans tend to avoid incongruity between their beliefs and their actions, was recognized by mass marketers as an important phenomenon. Mass advertising of automobiles, for example, was undertaken as much to reassure purchasers that they had done the right thing as to sell directly.

APPLYING THE THEORY

During the late 1960s there was a blossoming of understanding that could now be directly applied to the business world rather than remain within the realms of academia. The consumer was being seen as an organism that could be to some extent manipulated by advertising and marketing. In the same way, workers were being viewed mechanistically as a resource that could be honed and fashioned with motivational techniques to create higher efficiency. Victor Vroom (*Work and Motivation*, 1964[2]) and J.W. Atkinson (*A Theory of Achievement Motivation*, 1966[3]) led the charge, looking at the importance of the work environment and the effectiveness of money as an incentive device for higher productivity (or not, as it turned out).

There was great debate during the 1970s and 1980s about job satisfaction and expectations of employees, no doubt fuelled by two major recessions that added to the body of work about how people at work are motivated to improve their performance, regardless of how the market is doing. In particular some pioneering work was achieved in the area of goal setting, both for individuals and groups. However, what was missing from a sales management point of view was any unified theory of individual or group motivation that could be applied to salespeople in a commercial environment.

In 1992, the answer came with Martin Ford's Motivational Systems Theory. Published as *Motivating Humans*[4] the book covered the entire history of incentive and motivational research, with an all-embracing theory of human motivation with some useful commercial applications for sales managers. The basic summary is as follows:

$$\text{Achievement (job competence)} = \frac{\text{Motivation} \times \text{skill} \times \text{responsive environment}}{\text{Biology}}$$

Ford lists the 17 principles of human motivation which, when applied to sales situations, and the development of incentive schemes, all have a degree of common sense.

Some of Ford's general principles

1. The Principle of Unitary Functioning: see the big picture and consider all the ramifications.
2. The Triumvirate Principle: combine goals, emotions and personal attitude.
3. The Principle of Goal Activation: make goals relevant to the task.
4. The Principle of Goal Salience: make multiple goals complementary, not in conflict with each other.
5. The Feedback Principle: provide regular feedback on desired performance.
6. The Flexible Standards Principle: relate standards to past performance, make them achievable.
7. The Optimal Challenge Principle: set difficult but do-able targets.
8. The Reality Principle: ensure participants have the skills to do what is required.
9. The Principle of Emotional Activation: promote the program with emotion not logic.
10. The Principle of Incremental Change: ask for relatively small changes in performance, rather than step changes.

It is clear from these principles that have strong experimental findings to support them, that any incentive or reward scheme for salespeople will work more efficiently if these principles and other motivational theories are borne in mind.

TIMELINE (YEAR:THEORIST – ISSUE)

- **1901**: Freud – The psychopathy of everyday life
- **1912**: Jung – Extroverts and introverts
- **1938**: Murray – Twenty basic human needs
- **1943**: Maslow – Hierarchy of needs
- **1959**: Herzberg – Satisfiers and dissatisfiers
- **1964**: Vroom – Work and motivation
- **1966**: Atkinson – The need for achievement
- **1975**: Latham – High performance goal setting
- **1991**: Cantor – Importance of goals and emotions
- **1992**: Ford – Motivational systems theory

PRACTICAL EXAMPLES

Example one

You are the sales manager of a financial services company. You have a salaried sales force that is paid a bonus on the year-end profits of the whole organization, including the administration team. Your average sales performers seem quite happy to plod along at their own pace but you have noticed a rise in leavers from the top quartile to your main competitor, even though you have offered many individuals an extra payment to stay. Sales have risen in line with inflation but no higher and much less than sales of competitors. What should you do?

It is clear from the description that the average salesperson is not being stretched enough. We know from Atkinson that people are driven to achieve through the conflict between hope and fear. Individuals make choices between the hopes for success and fears of failure. In this case there are no apparent corporate sanctions for failure so individuals simply "plod along." We also know from Freud that there is a trade-off between pain and pleasure and every individual makes a judgment about the reward value of working harder. There is no incentive to work harder so the average salesperson simply relaxes. You need to introduce an individual target that stretches the individual to their limit while still being perceived as attainable and offer incremental rewards for gradual ongoing sales achievement. To focus attention on the sales role they should be taken out of the overall company bonus scheme with the budget being used for incentivizing incremental sales for those who perform.

The high fliers are bored. Using our knowledge of Maslow we can see that they have gone beyond their comfort zone in earnings and are looking for a bigger challenge. They would respond well to an "honors club" which would provide status within a group of like-minded individuals and allow opportunities for peer-group recognition. At the very top end a gold level could be established which would offer leading-edge training, contact with senior staff management and company-wide recognition for any contributions they make above and beyond pure sales.

Example two

An automotive manufacturer has a well-known brand of family saloon and has run incentives for its salespeople for many years. They are used to competition and being ranked in order of sales performance. This year for the first time the company decides to run a similar scheme for staff in its after-sales departments. Individuals are monitored by their bosses for general performance levels and low level cash payments are made to those who are deemed by their manager to have done a better than average job during the campaign period. The program bombs and nobody is sure why. Management reckons they have wasted their money and refuse to do it again, keeping their budget for the sales team. Is this what you would do?

This scheme falls foul of at least one of Ford's principles of motivation, namely that of *Unitary Functioning*. What works for one section of the organization may be totally inappropriate for another part. The after-sales people have had no experience of incentive campaigns before, and they do not know what is expected of them to become successful. The mechanism for measuring individual performance seems very arbitrary and the rewards are probably too low for participants to cross the pain/pleasure threshold. The result is a withdrawal of cooperation and a nasty taste in everyone's mouth.

A better way forward would have been to find measures of team performance that would be acceptable such as the efficiency of services undertaken, customer satisfaction or hygiene factors in the workplace. Having established that these were activities that could be improved, reasonable but stretching standards could be set in return for an attractive reward, including non-cash elements. The better performing teams would be highlighted in the company newsletter and the top team in the network would be invited to meet the national bosses at their headquarters and spend a night on the town, hosted by the organization.

Example three

A major IT software company operates through a series of local distributors who then sell on to retailers. The supplier wants to get more sales through the retail outlets of its products but so far it has only been able to do so using high profile sales promotion and brand advertising. The new sales director decides to circumvent the power of the distributors and starts collecting salespeople's names through his field force with a view to offering a lavish travel incentive to the top retail salespeople. When the six distributors find out, they cancel the manufacturer's contracts and refuse to allow any of their products into any of their retail outlets. What did the sales director do wrong?

There was nothing wrong with the wish to offer incentives directly to those with the ability to improve their performance but the sales director ignored the cultural environment in which the industry operates. In this case the first job is to motivate the distributors to want to allow the supplier a closer relationship with their distribution network. The incentive plan should have included a hospitality and relationship-building campaign for the distributors with practical marketing and training support for the retailers they represent. Once the supplier had established, say, a "club" for the retailers' staff based on technical fluency with the product, he could then seek permission to run performance-based incentives as part of the overall scheme. Distributors could be tied in with incentives for the distributor to encourage their own retailers to become more involved.

For a more detailed explanation of what structure to use in any given situation see Chapter 6, The State of the Art.

HOLISTIC APPROACH

It is not unusual for sales managers to use tried and tested management techniques when confronted with similar problems. Some rely on the fear factor of sanctions to motivate their team. Others heap rewards on everyone in the hope that some of it may work. Still more lurch from one technique to another as each year goes by, expecting to discover by chance the best way to get more performance from their particular salespeople. None of these options is correct in isolation. What the history of human motivation and incentive theory tells us is that there are many interlocking and well-researched facts about human motivation which, when applied in the right circumstances, will produce predictably good results. Ford's Motivational Systems Theory is nothing more than applied research into what works and what does not when it comes to getting the best out of human beings as individuals. There is still a lot of research to be done when it comes to understanding how individuals can be best motivated within a group context.

KEY LEARNING POINTS

- Research into human motivation only began at the turn of the twentieth century and concentrated on what caused individuals to do what they do.
- By the 1950s social scientists turned their attention to the workplace and established a number of key facts about incentives and rewards in a commercial context.
- In the 1990s a number of different findings were gathered together under an overall framework by Martin Ford called the Motivational Systems Theory.
- Group motivation studies are still in their infancy and much remains to be established about how groups are motivated within the working environment.

» The best incentive schemes reflect a balanced scorecard of motivational principles that are now established and to some extent scientifically predictive.

NOTES

1 Murray, H. (1938) *Explorations in Personality*, Oxford University Press, New York.
2 Vroom, Victor H. (1964) *Work and Motivation*, John Wiley, New York.
3 Atkinson, J.W. (1966) *A Theory of Achievement Motivation*. Krieger Publishing Company, Florida.
4 Ford, Martin E. (1992) *Motivating Humans*, Sage Publications, California.

12.07.04

The E-Dimension

- Measuring performance
- Mirroring
- Reward fulfillment
- Telemetry
- Best practice, IBM case history
- Key learning points

> "The compelling and main reason for e-commerce is simply and ultimately more revenue ... it's all about sales. It's about really supporting sales, so there's an added requirement of a lot of communication among IT, marketing, sales and others."
> *Aaron Goldberg, vice president and principal analyst, Ziff Davis*

What makes the Internet such a revolutionary business tool is the speed at which information can now be exchanged between individuals. Government agencies and large corporations were the first to benefit as they were the only organizations that could afford their own networks and servers. Initially the new technology was being used to leverage better buying power by channeling all their purchasing through a single point. Electronic Data Interchange or EDI as it is known, replaced the cumbersome system of sending data tapes around the offices to be able to analyze sales and distribution on a large scale. By the early 1990s, by using HTML and Mosaic Web formats both text and graphics could be exchanged on a global basis at astonishing speed. General Electric was one of the early pioneers with its Trading Post procurement system.

But the key advantage for sales organizations was the new ability to set robust measures of sales performance and be able to monitor individual achievement on a daily basis via the Internet, rather than weekly or even monthly. Although most reward and incentive schemes are still managed through paper and printed reporting procedures, all the major users have moved to electronic data management and communication of results, when running sales incentive campaigns.

MEASURING PERFORMANCE

Incentive programs for salespeople rely on being able to set specific targets against which they can be measured. Typical measurements may include:

1. overall sales
2. sales of specific products
3. sales to specific clients
4. sales to new prospects
5. sales in specific distribution areas
6. service quality

7 merchandizing levels
8 prospecting activity
9 product knowledge
10 better administration/paperwork

Each of these measurements requires a high degree of data management input that needs to be accurate and timely if the sales incentive is going to be effective. The skills to collect data and store it in a useful format have been around for some time. Typically you would need to create a sales database that gives each salesperson a unique identifier. That identifying code would indicate fields such as length of service, current title of job, territory, current sales level, reporting structure and current sales target. Often these systems are hybrids of the payroll. However, in order to measure performance against new and often changing targets software needs to be written which applies the data management routines which can show who has done what. Writing sales software can be expensive so it is just as well to get it right first time around rather than having to amend the program each time you want to run an incentive.

So, having established individual records for each participant, you then need to create an incentive performance package from which you could pick and choose, depending on the incentive you want to run. For example, if you want to reward increase in performance, you need to have a routine that will calculate the percentage increase in what they do now, compared with what was done historically. You may wish to add timekeeping to the measure as one of the qualifiers for payments so you will need to have a file on each individual's time-keeping record. You may wish to reward according to their manager's rating, so you need a system which will collect and record that assessment against an individual salesperson's file and so on. In practice most incentive schemes include a mix of sales achieved and other activity to provide a rounded view of an individual's performance.

By running the individual file against the incentive program file, you can achieve a performance output file that could rank individuals by each measure or by a combination of measures, as appropriate. But what the Internet brings to cutting edge incentive programs is the speed of both data collection and data communication. In the bad old days, sales data would come in as a mixture of electronic files, manual payroll records and perhaps faxed reports from outlying offices. This process often took so long that telling participants how they were doing could only be done on a monthly basis and sometimes not as often as that.

Now, thanks to the speed of information exchange on the Internet, performance reports can be generated in just a few days. Measuring individual performance, however complex, with the right incentive program software, is achievable almost instantly and can help field managers on the ground spot operational problems much faster than before the Internet was commercially available. Poor performing representatives or difficult sales patches can be isolated within days rather than weeks so that remedial action can be taken quickly.

MIRRORING

But collecting sales performance data more quickly is only half the story. We know from Martin Ford's Feedback Principle, (see Chapter 3, The Evolution of Sales Rewards and Incentives), that performance improvement and motivation can be enhanced by telling participants how they are doing. Grass Roots, a European incentives agency, inherited a paper-based incentive program for telecoms provider British Telecom called Share in Success which had been running for six years. Call center staff were monitored across 35 locations against various sales and service measures but printed bulletins were costly and grossly out of date by the time participants received them, with a consequent loss of excitement and positive motivation. Bulletins were only sent out monthly.

The participant database was researched to reveal that over 80% considered that a switch to e-mail reporting would be a big improvement. The agency developed a Website that not only reported sales achievements on a daily basis but also linked participants to an online catalogue of over 2000 items, which they could redeem against points earned in the program. On average, participants logged on to the new sales incentive Website seven times a month to check on their own progress whereas before they only received paper bulletins monthly. The new program was renamed SHIN*e*, with the emphasis on e-mail based communication.

Campaign Websites have now become the standard way to launch new incentive and reward campaigns. They can either be set up as an addition to the client's own Website or as a stand-alone site, administrated by an agency or promotions house. Participants access the campaign Website via a password and often have restricted access to their own or their peer group's performance. Clients will be sensitive to any public airing of internal sales data so anyone offering to set up a campaign Website needs to be properly vetted for security and data retrieval capabilities.

REWARD FULFILLMENT

As in the example above, the next enhancement provided by the Internet is the ability to offer participants the facility to redeem their rewards instantly by e-mail rather than have to complete onerous paperwork and then have to wait for the sponsor to confirm by mail that they have qualified.

Before e-mail was commonly available it was normal for winners in incentive campaigns to complete a claiming procedure to claim their awards. Claimants would discover they had won something, from a paper-based bulletin. They then had to claim the item by post after completing an administration form, normally endorsed by the line manager. The procedure undertaken by the administration team could be quite complex. Claim forms would be entered into a central database to verify the claim and the claimant's details. Often the list of verified claimants would then go out to managers in the field so they could double-check for any discrepancies. Once approved the instruction would go out to the reward supplier as to what to send where. In the case of retail vouchers or bonds this would simply be a mail exercise, although postal proof that the vouchers had been received would be needed to avoid double-redemptions. In the case of merchandise, if the supplier only fulfilled orders once a week or once a fortnight, there could be a considerable delay built in to the process of receiving rewards. As for rewards dealing with individual travel, the routine often involved the nominated supplier contacting the winners to discuss with them directly what type of holiday they required. It would not have been unusual for winners to have to wait at least a month for their reward to arrive.

With the Internet the onerous, time-wasting and costly administration of incentive schemes has largely disappeared for those who use the technology now available. Potential winners' details can be sent via EDI to the administrators of the scheme for verification. Within seconds the winner and his or her line manager can be notified by e-mail of what they have won. Subject to the rules of the campaign the winners can then choose their reward online which can be re-routed directly to the reward suppliers. Sometimes points can be added to reward credit cards electronically which winners then redeem through local retail outlets for goods and services which are in the redemption scheme. US performance improvement specialist Maritz has developed Exclusively Yours, a hybrid Mastercard. It functions like a standard credit card and provides winners with fast and easy access to their rewards through nominated retailers. There are a number of other systems around the world serving local markets that now largely eliminate the need for paper-based reward redemption, thanks to the Internet

TELEMETRY

Telemetry is the science of measuring from a distance. Used extensively in the military for calculating the distance of targets it has now come to mean, in marketing circles, the measurement of performance by electronic means. The impact of the Internet on distance measurement has been revolutionary. Standard reporting cycles have been cut from weeks to days and even hours thanks to e-mail and EDI. As a result incentives are now being directed more and more to activities within the sales process rather than the end result. Every sales manager knows that if sellers are active, they will create sales. It's a numbers game, as they say. The more calls you make, the more appointments you get. The more appointments you get, the more presentations you can do. The more presentations you do, the more confirmed sales you make. All aspects of the prospecting process can now be analyzed in minute detail that provides the "motivational interventionist" with the opportunity to reward desired behavior at every stage. Successful sales calls can now be rewarded instantly and online, providing the motivation to improve on hit rates as the working day progresses. A by-product is the ongoing report on performance for managers so they can see who is working well, what scripts are working best and what kind of deals are being done. For those who rely on high turnover and reaching new customers, telemetry can provide sales performance measurement in minute and continuous detail that would have been impossible without the Internet.

BEST PRACTICE

To conclude this section here is an example of how a traditional and long-time user of incentives has used the Internet to its best advantage when planning its distributor and reseller incentive programs for the twenty-first century.

CASE STUDY: IBM's CIRCLE OF SUCCESS

During 2001 IBM's eServer division was launching the next generation of server products. One of the objectives was the positive involvement and support of all its distributors and third party resellers. There was an existing scheme called Circle of Success, which had just 600 local market, registered participants and was largely print-based in its communication plan. It was decided to use the Web to gather more participants rather than using direct mail, as it was considered the most cost-effective way to get more involvement. The Internet-linked invitation process produced a 250% increase in registered participants, bringing the number to 1500 in total at a fraction of the snail-mail cost.

Once on board, all the registered participants were given access to a newly created Website, Circle of Success, as the main means of communicating details of a new suite of products in the xSeries range. Hyperlinks to other IBM sites were created as part of the site so that participants in the program could find detailed support when required whenever they logged on.

Participants earned points for every sale made during the annual campaign. Points could be collected by individuals or pooled for the entire reseller business. Each quarter specific xSeries products were given varying points levels to stimulate certain types of sale. All points achieved were credited and validated within 48 hours and posted online. Every two weeks e-shots were sent with campaign news, product enhancements and seasonal reward offers. Click-thru rates increased significantly following each e-shot.

Participants were encouraged to spend their reward points online through a password mechanism on the Circle of Success site. They included retail vouchers, merchandise, holidays, lifestyle activities, or even business-related items such as branded merchandise or extra IBM training modules. Individual or team credit updates were made available online so that participants could check their progress at any time, 24/7, during the campaign.

The results were astounding. An increase in sales through this channel of 42% was recorded with the added benefits of a much wider participation database and a firmer platform for future communication about the xSeries. Circle of Success Websites are now established as IBM's major channel of communication with its distributor/reseller network and it is hoped in the future to expand the site to other product groups and involve other IBM business partners such as Intel. Circle of Success is a good example of how a simple incentive can become a major communication channel while still achieving the original intention of creating volume sales. In this case it is also a classic example of using the new Internet technology to deliver proven incentive campaign results with shorter lead times and savings on print and reward distribution costs.

KEY LEARNING POINTS

- Speed of information exchange has created a revolution in the administration of incentive and reward schemes. E-mail and Electronic Data Interface (EDI) has simplified the whole process of reporting sales performance.
- Communicating performance to participants in the incentive program can now be achieved instantly, helping to make the campaign more immediate and exciting.

- One of the principles of effective incentive schemes is the facility to provide the reward as closely as possible to the desired action. The Internet has provided the opportunity for rewards to be claimed instantly by winners and so helps to reinforce the objectives of the campaign more quickly.
- Telemetry or the facility to measure performance at a distance on a virtually continuous basis has created the opportunity to measure the minute detail of the sales process to the extent that activity as well as sales can be incentivized if required.
- New reward products have been created as a direct result of the Internet that allow participants to receive their rewards as soon as they have achieved the required action. The implications are that the incentive and reward schemes can now be fulfilled instantly, thereby reinforcing desired behavior in a more direct way than through paper-based administration processes.

12.07.05

The Global Dimension

- Regional schemes
- Cross-border programs
- Global incentives of the future
- Best practice examples
- Key learning points

"The world is disgracefully managed, one hardly knows to whom to complain."

Ronald Firbank, Edwardian novelist

Everyone is different. This is also true of commercial organizations and the people who work for them. The challenge for the "motivational interventionist" in today's business environment is to try to find a sales incentive program which can be successfully translated across national borders as more and more organizations are functioning on a regional or a global basis. However, there are a number of economic, cultural and conceptual issues to deal with when attempting to make "one size fit all."

REGIONAL SCHEMES

When an incentive program is successful in a defined geographical area it is natural to want to get some mileage from the inevitable set up costs and introduce the same scheme to another area. You will have learned all the pitfalls, paid for the database to work efficiently and have a pretty good idea of the likelihood of success. But is it simply a question of changing the names of the participants or having the material translated into a foreign language? There are a number of variables to consider:

» Same structure? You need to consider whether the distribution structure is the same in the new area as in the original area. Sometimes the same organization has different arrangements and procedures for doing business in other areas even when those areas are only separated by a hundred miles or so. The last thing you need in a professional sales organization is trouble with your distributors.
» Same targets? Economic yield often differs substantially from one area to the next, even within the same country. This is one reason why some sales areas are given different sales quotas even though they may have the same number of salespeople. You may need to consider a weighting system (see Chapter 6) to compensate for the lack of sales development potential.
» Same rewards? Offering an all-expenses-paid trip to the big city may not be overly attractive to those who already live there. Equally

a weekend at the beach may not go down too well for those participants who already live on the coast.

» Same products? Every sales organization has its own patterns of distribution for each of its products. It may well be that certain products always sell well in the south but rarely do well in the north. If you attempt to run a sales incentive and ignore these proven trends you may well find yourself giving an unfair advantage in sales terms to one portion of the participant database.
» Same communication? Although both areas may speak the same language, do they sell and service their clients in the same way? You may decide that a rurally based sales team may need a different tone of voice to one that is largely city-based. Should new recruits get the same messages as the old-stagers? Should specific product specialists get specific new product messages rather than the general round robin that everyone else gets?

Taken to its extreme, the best incentive program should be one in which the structure, communication and rewards are totally geared to the individual. However, just as with advertising, this would be too expensive to administer on a one-to-one basis. So we need to find an acceptable, commercial compromise that recognizes crucial differences but in essence is a generic program with some common themes. A simple example is the "beat-your-best" concept. All participants, regardless of sales territory or experience, can be rewarded with reference to their improvement in sales over and above what they did during the same period last year/month/week. However, you must introduce some minimum performance criteria.

CROSS-BORDER PROGRAMS

Taking a program cross-border is one of the biggest challenges facing incentive planners today. As globalization demands common treatments in marketing and communications, it is often assumed that the same principles can be applied to incentive programs, often with disastrous results. The main elements to consider are language, culture and being able to deliver the reward itself on an individual or group basis.

Language

Anyone acquainted with the Internet will be able to recount tales of the inadequacy of automatic translation devices for marketing texts. This is equally true of incentive copy. Even at the most basic level, the program title for example, it is virtually impossible to translate phrases such as: "mission: improvement" or "winner takes all." An interesting rendering into Spanish of a British teamwork incentive called "Today-Tomorrow-Together" produced the campaign theme, "Hoy-Manana-Juntos" which although correct, hardly carries the same cleverness as the English phrase. Another program called in English, "Breaking the Barriers" was translated as "Eliminando Barreras." Again, the translation is technically accurate but somehow fails to inspire in a sales context.

Beyond the overall theme there are a number of issues to do with sales phraseology that need careful thought before driving on to the launch sequence. Are you really convinced your foreign audience will understand terms such as "fast-start", "accumulator", "redemption hotline", or "all claims must be validated"?

Culture

A broader issue is one of culture. Within the niche world of incentive and performance improvement planning the business community seems to be divided between the Anglo-Saxons (US, UK, Australia and Canada) and everyone else. In general terms whatever is produced in one part of the English-speaking world will be acceptable in most others from concept and theme down to the rules and the rewards. However this is not the case in other countries. Non-cash incentives, as provided in the context of a sales campaign, are virtually unknown in the Far East and Eastern Europe where the distribution rules are very different and cash is still king. The relatively recent crackdown on organized crime in Italy has meant that for some multi-national corporations small scale incentives for purchasers or budget-holders are frowned upon and can lead to dismissal if accepted, although these corporations are a major user of organized and sponsored incentive travel within a business context.

Delivering the reward

A key issue with cross-border campaigns is the technical feasibility of being able to deliver any rewards won. Within a single political or geographic state you would use the normal national distribution channels. However, you will come across a number of barriers when trying to send merchandise items overseas. Many countries do not allow the import of alcohol or meat (such as food hampers) without a considerable tariff and others actively block the sending of electrical consumer goods unless they were originally made in that country to begin with. Your next thought may be to issue the winners with vouchers that they can redeem in local retail outlets up to a prescribed level. There is no such reward instrument available at present that is proven to be acceptable across borders apart from traveller's checks, although some incentive consultancies have tried to create a similar idea with variant versions of internationally acceptable credit cards.

Reward solutions

A major factor in the distribution of rewards to overseas participants is the cost. Often the postal or delivery charge far outweighs the actual cost of the item being sent. One solution is to arrange to have goods delivered locally from within the participant's own country, so the choice of reward needs to be available locally. If you are running a pan-Europe program with outlets in seven or eight countries, the administration costs could be enormous and far exceed any incremental benefit obtained from running the program in the first place. This leads inevitably to providing group travel as incentives because all the winners could easily travel to one place, although the destination chosen would have to be outside any of the countries in which the participants live.

GLOBAL INCENTIVES OF THE FUTURE

There is no doubt that the Internet will throw up some useful technology with which to solve the technical problems associated with programs which emanate from one country but which operate in many others. The issue of communication has all but been solved thanks to e-mail (see Chapter 4, The E-dimension) with translation of performance data now being relatively simple. Reward fulfillment is really just an administrative issue. The software being developed to create B2B ordering systems, first pioneered by General Electric in the early 1990s with its Trading Post procurement product, will help to create an online network of reward suppliers on a global basis who are situated locally, thereby removing the main problem of delivery. ASPs (Application Software Providers) relating to incentives are being developed by all the major incentive consultancies but it will not be long before they will be in a position to hire out their software for a license fee so that clients can run systems for themselves.

Another key issue is the relevance of certain types of reward for different cultures. We are not far from the time when a cross-border or global program may have a generic, global title such as Performance Matters but with rewards specific to each geographical region. In some cases the rewards may just be more cash. The top achievers in each area could still qualify for an overseas travel event in a neutral country and so add a second layer to the basic scheme. The result should be a program which meets the needs of every participating group in any global location, from targeted communication in the language of the participants right through to relevant and stretching rewards.

However, care needs to be taken not to produce a theme and program so bland and universal that it means nothing to those outside the inner circle of successful regions. As with all types of marketing there comes a point when the savings on origination and creativity are less important than getting the sales team enthusiastic and engaged. The most highly structured and researched global program is no good at all if it does not ultimately deliver improvements in the sales process.

BEST PRACTICE EXAMPLES

There are presently so few best practice examples of global or indeed cross-border programs that it would be misleading to present a single case history as it would not be typical. Instead, here are a few examples of how some organizations are, at the very least, tackling some of the issues and getting to grips with the major challenges.

Motorola

Motorola Inc is a Six-Sigma (the quality standards benchmarking system) company and is proud of the progress which was made in the US during the 1990s in its development of operational standards which were aligned to the strategic plan of the business. In the mid-1990s the organization decided to roll-out to its European network the US idea of an incentive scheme which rewarded successful completion of its agreed operational standards. After much discussion it was decided that a straightforward translation of the documentation into the seven or eight languages required to cover its EMEA region would not be sufficient. Various planning meetings were held which concluded that in general Northern Europe would be fine and the program could be handled in English but Southern Europe would need specific country translations and in some cases a change of concept. Not all employees accept that the US way is necessarily the best. It was also agreed that the cost of tracking individual compliance to the standard procedures in the business would be far too expensive and difficult to monitor in a robust way. For that reason a nomination system was adopted for Europe in which "good operational compliance examples" were eligible for votes from peers in the business and the individuals with the most nominations were awarded prizes. Those at the very top of their regional tree of achievement were invited to the Motorola University in Chicago to meet senior corporate officers, invited on a tour of the manufacturing plant and rounded off with a Caribbean cruise before flying back to Europe.

Fiat Auto

Fiat Auto runs a complex series of sales incentive programs in virtually all its major markets. Within the UK, for example, there are schemes for dealers, sales managers, after sales managers, service engineers and showroom staff. The same structure is repeated in Germany, Italy and the Netherlands to name but a few. But each country has total autonomy on how each program is constructed, the communication platform, the rewards and the management of the performance data. The quality of each country's program varies simply because some countries have better services within the marketing sector for delivering and administrating such schemes. As far as head office in Turin is concerned, as long as the schemes deliver higher sales, there is no need to become involved in the minutiae of the campaigns. Clearly it helps from time to time to run best practice meetings to see if countries can learn from each other's experiences and perhaps make fewer mistakes but in general each country does its own thing and lives or dies by its knowledge of the local market and how it will respond.

Rolls Royce Cars

Rolls Royce Cars had exactly the opposite incentive dilemma. With fewer than a hundred showrooms worldwide they wanted to create a competitive element within their network on a global basis regarding sales even though units per dealership sold per month rarely went into double digits. It would be costly to create the administration of an incentive scheme for each region in the world as the room for improvement was relatively small. So they opted for an incentive travel event to which all dealerships were enrolled. Dealers competed for six months against an agreed local target and the top dealers and their partners were invited to London to compete in the London to Monte Carlo rally, using Rolls Royce cars and staying for the overnight stays in Relais Chateaux properties. The event culminated in a gala dinner at the Hotel de Paris, in the center of Monaco, where further prizes were awarded for performance in the rally, with the added bonus of local television crews covering stages of the rally as the cars swept through rural France. The uplift in sales remains confidential but it is sufficient to say that it proved to be one of their best-ever years for conquest sales (sales to new customers) and created a valuable communication channel into the dealer showroom staff that until then had never been exploited.

KEY LEARNING POINTS

- As large organizations become more global in their operations, sales rewards and incentives need to be created which are both culturally acceptable and effective.
- Advances in Internet technology will help in the administration of such programs in the future but for the moment examples of global schemes that work well are few and far between.

- Sponsors need to decide whether to be hands-on or hands-off when it comes to managing schemes in other regions or countries.
- Setting out the agenda and then letting local management run local programs is the best way to get an effective return on your incentive investment.

12.07.06

The State of the Art

» Guiding principles
» Human audit
» Some examples
» Skills assessment
» Communication
» The media mix
» Reward choices
» Setting objectives
» Creating effective programs
» Structural ideas
» Strategic incentives
» Likely trends and developments
» Key learning points

> "Measurements are powerful motivators. Companies measure what they value, sending employees clear signals about what is important. Measurements guide a variety of decisions, including where to focus product development efforts, what training to offer and what to reward."
>
> *Guy Schoenecker, president, BI Inc*

Sales rewards and incentives have come a long way from the merchandize catalogues of the 1940s and 1950s, although most non-specialists these days still equate offering consumer goods as prizes with incentive schemes. It is true that smaller organizations still use catalogues and retail vouchers as the best value alternative to bespoke incentive campaigns but most serious users in the US and Northern Europe have moved into the more sophisticated arena of performance improvement. Do this, get that has been replaced by an analytical approach to the process behind effective sales management in order to improve the component parts. Simply encouraging the sales team by force of personality to try harder is no longer enough. Contemporary sales incentive programs are often thoroughly researched and meticulously tracked as a marketing tool and take advantage of all the current psychological theories behind individual and group motivation within a commercial context.

GUIDING PRINCIPLES

A number of the world's major performance improvement consultancies have tried to encapsulate their advisory service in a simple model. Maritz, the largest US firm, uses a wheel graphic called The Maritz Performance Improvement System, listing consultancy services such as gap closure, awareness, implementation and reinforcement studies. This research would lead to decisions on which products to use, such as holding a meeting, setting up a database or running a customer satisfaction program. The management of the program would involve reward/recognition, skill development, measurement, assessment and communications. Other agencies include more or fewer services depending on their own agency offering. But all the published models of how to begin the process of performance improvement

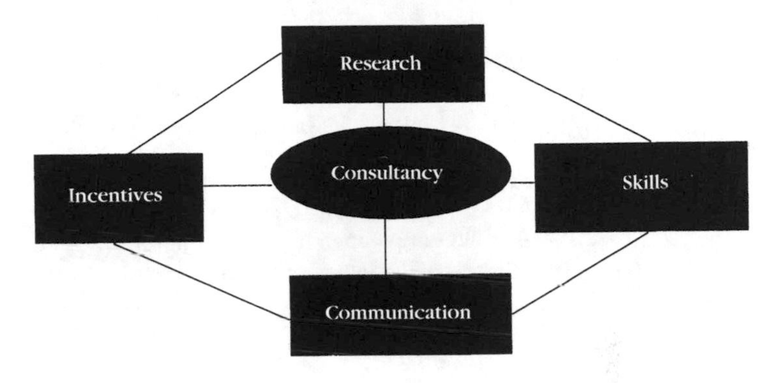

Fig. 6.1 Performance improvement model.

include the four key elements of research, skills level, communication and rewards. (See Fig. 6.1.)

The performance improvement model is a virtuous circle for any incentive or performance issue. Providing you address each of these four elements and take advice on each one, constructing an effective program should be straightforward.

THE HUMAN AUDIT

As you can see from Figure 6.1 the first task in a serious performance improvement program is to research the sponsor's business environment and the participant database. Sometimes known as the human audit this first phase gathers together detailed information about the sponsor's trading position within its own market, the role of the groups of people in its organization in terms of its success, and a listing of any promotional/incentive schemes which have been tried before, together with any objective results. Typically this stage begins with desk research including the statistics and budgets of past programs, informal interviews with sales or human resources management, and soundings amongst the participants about what has worked and what has not. This can be quite difficult, as most organizations do not keep robust records of such initiatives.

The next stage is a formal research project undertaken by an independent, external agency to establish the main issues. It is vital that this research is carried out by an objective team as cultural issues within organizations can easily skew any results obtained. Recorded discussions with senior management and selected groups of participants lead to the emergence of a clear list of issues to be addressed. However, focus groups are rarely predictive of the strength of feeling on each issue. For that reason a statistically valid sample then needs to be approached on an anonymous basis to discover the depth of feeling. This may be up to 25% of the whole participant database. The key findings are likely to revolve around inadequate communication and a mismatch between what management thinks and what the ordinary participants think. Part of the process may involve floating any number of possible "incentive solutions" to the participant sample to obtain a measure of what would be acceptable in the future. In essence the research should write the new program for you, without having to run a pilot test.

SOME EXAMPLES

Prudential Assurance had been running travel incentives for many years to motivate their top salespeople. However, the number of winners was relatively small compared to the size of the entire sales force. They decided to do a human audit and discovered that if they were to take fewer people to the overseas convention and used the money saved to motivate the middle-band of achievers with domestic weekend events in hotels, the change would be well received and broadly supported. The program was changed the following year and was a resounding success.

Things do not always run smoothly. It may be that the very process of researching participants' opinions throws up some deeper issues that an incentive scheme will not solve on its own. GDA, part of General Electric in Europe, undertook an extensive human audit of its 1200 service engineers who attended call-outs from customers whose washing machines were faulty or simply needed servicing. A complex series of interviews and questionnaires was distributed over a two-month period and the results were clear. A non-cash incentive scheme to reward above average performance would both be well received and produce more incremental returns than continuing with the cash incentive they were currently running. However, the organization was about to undergo a change of financial ownership at the same time as it was testing the introduction of laptops for all its locally based service engineers. Despite the positive results of the research into a new approach to incentives it was felt that some time should be given to bedding in the new technology and the relationship with the new owners before going ahead with a major change in remuneration strategy.

SKILLS ASSESSMENT

One of the main concerns surrounding sales rewards and incentives is to make sure that the participants actually have the necessary skills to do their job better. No incentive in the world can compensate for better sales training and wider product knowledge. In fact in almost every case you would be wasting your resources if you introduced an incentive scheme without checking on the skills levels of those who are due to take part.

Take the example of an automotive dealer showroom sales representative. As the first point of contact for most customers who make their way eventually into a dealership, they need to have the right skills to empathize and obtain some customer details. It goes without saying that they need to know their current models and any deals that have been promoted in recent weeks. But they also need to be aware of any finance initiatives organized by their finance suppliers, and any after-sales offers currently being used, not to mention the dealer's current policy on part-exchange or pre-owned models. It would be pointless running an incentive based on getting customers to use the dealer's own finance company if the sales team were not fully briefed both on what the terms are and how to sell such deals to prospective buyers. Investing dealership cash into an incentive to encourage customers to bring their car in for a winter service, for example, would be less effective if the personnel who run the customer service desk are both unaware of the advertising and of the deal being offered.

On a broader level, organizations with large distributions may allocate promotional budgets to local salespeople to encourage their local distributors to do more business. If those local salespeople do not understand how to set up and run incentive programs themselves they are unlikely to be able to assess whether their local distributor is using the funding wisely. Simply writing a check to a local distributor for "incentives" is unlikely to produce any incremental return by itself and may simply find its way into the distributor's bank account to supplement their overhead costs with no benefit to the sponsor.

COMMUNICATION

Of all the possible issues that the human audit may throw up, communication, or the lack of it, is likely to be a major one. Sales organizations tend to be excellent at verbal communication and one-to-one coaching but less good with remote communication. The skills required are marketing skills such as graphic design, knowledge of print formats, direct mail, e-marketing, poster production and database management. Most research comments reveal a general lack of creativity when it comes to communicating incentives, a "launch-it-and-leave-it" attitude to ongoing promotion and a lack of follow-up when revealing the winners and the administrative arrangements for the distribution of rewards. The reason why such findings occur again and again is because promotional marketing to your own people rarely falls into a recognized category. Is it a sales management job or a marketing job? Should it be given to human resources? What about a local design agency? Whatever the analysis it needs to be treated as a real issue that needs to be managed. Most large organizations sub-contract the communication aspects to outside, specialist consultancies that are often able to help devise the best scheme and administrate the rewards. They are partly paid through time-based fees and through commissions on any rewards that are purchased on the sponsor's behalf so they have a vested interest in getting as many qualifiers as possible.

THE MEDIA MIX

Deciding what mix of communication media to use requires some thought. Promoting to a sales team could be as simple or as complicated as marketing to consumers. Possible media include:

» printed brochure
» wall chart
» e-mail
» newsletter

- single-sheet flyer
- payslip leaflet
- video
- intranet download
- teaser merchandize
- telephone messages
- team briefings
- personalized letters
- video conferencing
- sales convention
- on-target lunches
- mid-campaign drinks event
- text messages
- testimonials.

Each of these media will have an attached cost and an administrative element that should all be included in the sales incentive budget. It is also worth bearing in mind that although all potential participants should be included in the launch material, as the campaign progresses it may be more cost-effective to segment the participants into above-target, on-target and less-than-target groups so that the most expensive promotion can be directed at the group most likely to improve. Generally speaking, the middle band or the second and third quartile will have the largest capacity for improvement so this is the section to which most of the promotional effort should be directed.

REWARD CHOICES

The choice of which rewards to offer is rarely straightforward and almost always includes a number of different rewards for different levels of performance. Much research has been undertaken within a number of market sectors and types of sales organization to determine the best reward. In the 1990s the incentives consultants p&mm funded two research projects to determine the pecking order of rewards if the budget was no barrier. In both surveys of over 400 leading incentive users the ranking order of preference was the same. The results are given in Table 6.1.

Table 6.1 Order of preference for rewards. (Source: p&mm, UK.)

Reward	Percentage
Cash	43%
Overseas travel	35%
Retail vouchers	23%
Merchandise	20%
Weekend hotel trips	16%
Sports event tickets	14%

In general, after cash, individual or group travel concepts were deemed to be the most effective, followed by retail vouchers, specific items of merchandise, weekend hotel events and finally sporting events. Travel concepts work well as they are easy to promote and provide the opportunity to take the winners away as a hosted group, thereby improving morale and common purpose. By the same token tickets for national or local sporting events tend to be less successful as participants are given little time to interact with the hosts (they are there to watch the game) and if they are third party distributors often cannot remember who hosted them to any particular event.

However, this should not suggest travel is the only incentive that works. The cost of each travel reward can be very high in comparison to the additional performance achieved especially if the reward includes a ticket for the significant other with all taxes paid. This leads to the idea that most successful programs include a top tier of group travel rewards, a secondary tier of individual travel rewards and a third or further tier of lower denomination incentives such as retail vouchers or items of merchandise.

SETTING OBJECTIVES

Michael le Boeuf, professor of management at the University of New Orleans, said: "Reward people for the right behavior and you get the right results. Fail to reward the right behavior and you are likely to get the wrong results."

In sales, as in almost all parts of any organization, you need to be very clear what you want your people to do. Objectives work best, though, when you can isolate the desired behavior and tell people what degree of change is required. Setting sales objectives with defined targets is therefore crucial to the success of every incentive program. Here are some typical sales team objectives:

» increase sales
» increase specific product sales
» increase new prospect sales
» increase sales through specific channels
» increase sales in specific regions
» increase peripheral sales and services
» introduce new products/run out old models
» improve client retention
» improve the average sales value per customer
» respond to competitor activity
» improve call rates/activity
» recruit new salespeople
» test product knowledge.

Some of these objectives support each other, such as increasing specific product sales through new distribution channels. But take care not to run conflicting campaigns simultaneously through the same team, such as selling old products through a new channel at the same time as recruiting for new staff. It only leads to a lack of focus with salespeople not being sure what they are being asked to do.

The second point to consider is what level of performance would be both desirable and possible for each objective. You need to know what your team's performance would be without the injection of incentive funding. Calculate what percentage of improvement you need to cover the cost of the incentive, then add a reasonable return for the activity. In broad terms the calculations would be as follows.

CALCULATING THE PERCENTAGE IMPROVEMENT NEEDED

ABC Inc normally sells one million products. An incentive scheme is proposed to increase sales as market research shows that there is more demand in the market and competitors are selling more than they did this time last year.

1 Old hands in the sales department reckon that by offering an incentive they can increase their sales to 1.2 million over the campaign period, a 20% increase.
2 According to the finance department extra revenue from sales above budget earns profit at a 35% margin, so on $200,000 extra sales that would come to $70,000.
3 The marketing department says that it needs 33% of every incremental sale to pay for promotion, marketing and the incentives themselves. This equates to a cost of $23,100.
4 So, the incentive budget of $23,100 as a percentage of the incremental sales of $200,000 works out to 11.7%, in effect the break-even point.
5 As long as the incentive achieves at least an 11.7% increase, it will pay for itself. So the campaign target could be set at say 15% above budget to cover the costs and provide a contribution to the organization's profits.

This calculation can be done for any type of sales objective and a break-even point established. Any improvement above the break-even point is incremental profit. In practice well-managed sales incentives produce incremental sales of between 10% and 40% depending on the current trading conditions. It is always well worth creating several scenarios for the planned incentive campaign so that the finance department understands the implications of over-delivery as well as under-delivery. An incentive scheme that creates an incremental increase of 100% may be good news for the sales winners but less effective for the organization if the increase in products for delivery to customers cannot be achieved within a reasonable time-frame.

CREATING EFFECTIVE PROGRAMS

If the human audit has been completed correctly many elements of the program you introduce should write themselves. For example you will have discovered which types of reward appeal to which section of your participant database. You may even discover specific destinations that appeal to the top echelon. You will certainly discover how best to promote the program internally and even what theme would work best. So, having closed off the major unknowns the main task now is to structure the scheme in such a way that everyone will think they can win something, however token the rewards may be. All sales managers are aware that not everyone can be a top performer. The trick is to try and get most people to believe they can be. In other words the incentive budget is there as an investment to leverage better than expected sales performance. But where do you start?

Every large sales team follows a similar pattern of performance distribution. There is always a top tier of between 5% and 10% who consistently outperform the rest. They are long-term, professional salespeople who dedicate their lives to sales excellence and often involve their partners in their sales efforts too. The next 15% make up the balance of the top quartile and are high performing, committed individuals with the potential to become the very best in years to come. The next 25% are strivers who may have been with the organization for some years, intensely loyal and solid performers. The third quartile may be relatively new or alternatively very long-serving who may have reached their comfort zone and simply do not need to perform any higher. The bottom 25% are those who slipped through the recruitment net and may be considering moving out of the organization in the not too distant future.

The middle band of performers (those in the second and third quartiles) represent the main target for incentive programs as their collective capacity to improve performance far outweighs any aggregate improvement the top quartile by itself may achieve. The top quartile does have a part to play though. They provide role models for lesser performers and should be encouraged to "tell people how they became successful" through the communication plan. For those reasons the bulk of the budget and the promotion should go towards supporting and encouraging the middle band. This leads to a structure perhaps of an elite, hosted incentive travel event for the top 10% with individual travel awards for the remaining performers in the top quartile. The next two quartiles would be rewarded with retail vouchers and/or merchandise on an incremental basis, i.e. every time they improve their performance they receive rewards in proportion. The lowest quartile would receive encouraging promotion and perhaps a low level reward for their first achievement/gradation of improvement. Clearly each situation is different and the past use of incentives will play a part in determining what mix of rewards to use, and how to promote the program creatively.

STRUCTURAL IDEAS

Often there are specific objectives for each incentive campaign that can be enhanced by a clever approach to setting up the competitive groups or how the achievement points are won. Here are a few examples:

1 Put dealers into leagues so that they compete with peers. Often a small number of large volume dealer leagues and a larger number of smaller dealer leagues helps to even up the distribution of rewards if you are offering one big award for the top performer in each league. You can always have differing sizes of leagues to give the more important dealers a better statistical chance of winning.
2 Don't pay anything out until the target is reached (to cover your set up costs) then offer an escalating structure of rewards so that the more the participants do, the more reward they get.
3 If budgets are tight use a sweepstake system where every sale could be entered into a draw at the end of the campaign for major prizes. The more individual sales the participants do, the greater their chance of winning.
4 Create double-points for the first few weeks of the campaign to encourage participation and early involvement, otherwise known as a "fast-start."
5 Offer sales team rewards as well as individual rewards to encourage assisted sales.
6 Rank salespeople according to their contribution towards the entire sales target and reward them in proportion to their achievements.

Each technique will depend on the specific situation and market but try not to be too clever. If the scheme cannot be explained in a single sentence then it will be too complicated to explain to participants and they will simply turn off and not support the program.

STRATEGIC INCENTIVES

Many established users of sales incentive programs plan their incentive activities several years ahead to the extent that they become strategic. A budget is set at the beginning of the year for incentive activity. Typically there will be an annual program to cover performance improvement over the business year with honors clubs being devised to recognize as well as reward top organizational performance. Running parallel to the year-long program will be a number of two or three month tactical schemes to address particular issues within the sales year or in specific divisions. Within the automotive industry this could be a sales guild that runs for 12 months resulting in a dealer trip to Hawaii. Running simultaneously, the sales managers of the successful dealerships may be rewarded with a trip to London. During the year there may be a sales incentive for showroom salespeople on unit sales to retail customers or an after-sales merchandise catalogue scheme for achieving parts and accessory sales above target. Often manufacturers sponsor the administration and marketing of a quality standards program which operates at all levels of the franchise and pays out a cash override on the successful achievement of manufacturer-required service standards.

LIKELY TRENDS AND DEVELOPMENTS

There is no doubt that the biggest users of strategic incentive programs are the rich industrialized nations of the West. The problem is that as society becomes wealthier it is more and more difficult to find suitable rewards that are not commonplace. In the 1950s electrical consumer goods were only just becoming available to ordinary households. This explains why merchandise catalogues were the mainstay of many incentive programs until at least the late 1960s. Once successful salespeople had acquired all the gadgets on offer, travel was the next status measure for most people. Being able to say that you were off to some far-flung destination with your organization two or three times a year with your partner, all expenses paid, was a major benefit and something that promoted loyalty and retention. Now that overseas travel is more normal for many households attention has turned to more individual benefits such as golf or country club membership, lifestyle coaches, invitations to exclusive events and recognition devices. The recent growth in flexible benefits plans as part of the remuneration package also suggests that in the future incentive programs will result in more personalized rewards in which the winner spends the reward points in a variety of ways not necessarily as part of a corporate group.

Another factor that may militate against the effectiveness of incentives is the growth in applying tax to any awards taken. In the US, the EC, Australia and Canada the tax authorities have already set up departments to deal with the taxation of incentive benefits on a national basis. Monies are collected on behalf of the individual through the sponsoring organizations as soon as the programs are completed, so they have become a business expense that normally appears in the marketing budget. The days of being able to bury the cost are long gone.

The acid test of any sales incentive remains whether it can produce returns above and beyond its costs, even when you include the tax on the rewards themselves. It is becoming harder and harder to stay above that break-even line but with good communication and attention to detail it is one of few marketing techniques that can almost guarantee a cash-positive result with relatively little outlay.

KEY LEARNING POINTS

- The Performance Improvement Model (Fig. 6.1) provides a useful snapshot of what issues to consider when setting up a sales incentive scheme. Communication is often the critical issue.
- When setting objectives you need to establish non-conflicting goals and assign specific performance measures to them so that you can see what has been achieved at what cost. The human audit will help you uncover what the real issues are.
- Effective programs match the reward to the type of participant. Rewards could be travel, retail vouchers, merchandise, tickets to sporting events and more recently personalized rewards chosen by the individual winner.

- There are a number of structural ideas you can introduce into your plan to ensure you get the best return on your investment.
- Creating attractive sales incentives in the future is becoming more difficult as living standards increase and the tax authorities take their share of tax on rewards. But as long as there is an incremental benefit to the organization, they will continue to be an essential tool in the motivation of above average salespeople.

In Practice

- Categories of sales incentive programs
- Automotive
- White goods
- Retail
- Distress services
- Financial services - honors club
- Electrical retail goods
- Most likely users of travel
- Cyclical nature of incentives
- Human audit research
- Learning from experience

"Success is a science; if you have the conditions, you get the result."

Oscar Wilde, letter, 1883

Creating successful sales incentives and reward schemes is more science than art. Profitable programs do not happen by accident. They are the careful application of tried and trusted techniques. If by science we mean knowledge then one of the surest ways to feel confident that you are putting together a program that will work is to look at what other people have done. Every organization and its circumstances are different but there are some principles which stand out and transcend market sectors and the business cycle (see Chapter 6, The State of the Art). The following examples and case histories show how, with good planning and adjusting the principles to a specific sector, you can create incremental sales and other improvements from sales incentive and reward schemes.

These examples tackle a variety of issues but they all fall into a number of recognizable categories.

Increasing sales

The most used and therefore most talked-about sales incentive programs are those that aim to increase sales. They could be based on absolute sales increase or this quarter compared with last quarter. But usually because each product has its own sales season comparisons, such programs are best done on the basis of this period this year against the same period last year. But you do not always have to apply a percentage measure. You could compare actual sales volumes. In other words one hundred items more rather than so much revenue more. Or you could choose to use average sales per customer as the measure. Each one of these measures has a different outcome, especially regarding their perception by the participants, so take care when setting out the rules and walk through in your own mind who is likely to win based on the specific criteria you have chosen.

Learning new skills

Skills development is a key part in the growth of any seller. Once a salesperson has mastered the art of basic prospecting and presenting, future success will depend on the speed and degree of learning by the individual. This might include new products, new systems or new sales techniques. Inevitably acquiring new skills can seem boring and a waste of time to highly active entrepreneur types. Targeted incentive programs can fast track the higher performing sellers into more lucrative customer databases and provide an additional source of reward. Reward points can be offered for successful completion of various training modules with additional points for better than average achievement. Such incentive schemes work well when the sponsor needs to launch a new product or sell out an old product but team members are lacking the basic technical knowledge to sell the products successfully.

Loyalty

Retaining good salespeople can be a crucial issue when you need to grow your distribution quickly. You can spend as much time managing those you have hired as recruiting those you would like to have as new members of the sales effort. Honors clubs are a very effective way to provide reasons for old-timers to stay and to attract new recruits as part of an overall remuneration package. You may also consider phasing annual incentive events to a later stage of the newly entered sales year so as to retain their loyalty for longer. By the time they have enjoyed the fruits of last year's labors they are well into the following year's incentive program and therefore may think twice about looking for a new position outside the organization

Back-office skills

No sensible sales manager would expect the best salespeople to be excellent at back-office administration. But a lot of time and resources can be wasted correcting basic office procedures which need to be followed if the customer is to be well served and in some industries to satisfy the regulators that the right processes have been completed. Incentive schemes can be used to clean up administrative systems and reward compliance amongst salespeople to keep costs down. "Right First Time" programs should be part of every sales manager's plan to ensure the right products are sold to the right people at the appropriate time.

AUTOMOTIVE DEALER INCENTIVE (VOLVO)

During the 1980s Volvo, like almost all other automotive manufacturers in the world, offered cash payments to the owners of dealerships that performed at or above the manufacturer's sales plan. It was a mutually beneficial arrangement. The manufacturer could rely on the efficient dispatch of wholesale orders and the retailer (dealer) could rely on bonus payments with minimal effort. However, the world was changing. Car sales were running ahead of market demand and manufacturers had to position their products to ever-developing niches to maintain sales. In particular the smaller manufacturers from overseas were less able to buy their way into local markets. They had to market themselves differently.

Volvo, as a specialist supplier, realized that to get more Volvos into consumers' hands they would have to change radically the way their dealers were incentivized. They decided to experiment with non-cash incentives. They offered the owners of their franchises an opportunity to be hosted with their significant other for a private charter of the recently refurbished Venice Simplon Orient Express. Out of 250 dealers, 50 places were offered based on unit sales increase compared with the manufacturer's target. The sales managers who were employed by the franchise owner were offered retail vouchers for each unit sold. These non-cash incentives were in addition to the previously agreed cash bonuses for over-achieving against target. A three month incentive was devised called "The Sales Express" and promoted with a lavish brochure about the Orient Express train and Venice as a destination. The dealers were split into 50 leagues of 5 so that each dealer had a one in five chance of winning. To get the campaign off to a flying start, sets of Orient Express luggage were offered to any dealership which could achieve 50% of the campaign target by the end of the first month, otherwise known as a "fast-start."

The campaign made a big impression. Car sales during the period, in terms of local market share, rose from 2.66% to 4.74%, providing the importers, Lex Group, with their highest ever market share. Year on year comparative figures showed that sales had increased by 23%. The *Financial Times* covered the extraordinary leap in sales with an article, "Incentives help Volvo reach record sales", and credited the incentive campaign as being the main reason for the improvement in market penetration. From that period onwards, Volvo began to develop and refine non-cash incentives at all levels of the organization and managed to establish itself as having a reputation for delivering volume sales for the importer even though their marketing spend remains comparatively low compared with other higher profile, more local manufacturers.

KEY INSIGHTS

The Volvo campaign shows that in order to create extra leverage you need to think outside the norm–in this case, consider non-cash where cash has been the usual and expected reward mechanism. Those organizations that do try new techniques tend to get a "new-adopters bonus" in terms of a much better than expected increase in performance. This then has to be maintained as participants become accustomed to the new way of running programs.

WHITE GOODS (AEG)

AEG, the German producer of washing machines, dishwashers and dryers, had been running purchase-based incentives for many years, not unlike the Volvo example above but with merchandise as the reward. A catalogue was duly handed out at the beginning of each buying season and buyers would choose their items from the catalogue, provided they signed up for a certain volume of product. Over the years the scheme became tired and take-up began to dwindle. Only a handful of the top retailers ever claimed anything substantial. It seemed that the awards were just too thinly spread to be an attractive feature of the deal. In promotional terms, there was very little to talk about.

After an analysis of the distribution network it was clear that only 25% were buying enough stock to merit their being nominated as a specialist retailer. Providing market coverage and support to the entire network was becoming increasingly expensive. Not surprisingly, further analysis revealed that the top 25% produced 85% of the sales. It was decided that only the top echelon of 25% of retailers would be included in the non-cash program in the future and that they would have to compete for awards rather than just claim them as part of the purchasing process. The retailers were split into leagues where they would compete with businesses of a similar size. Fixed places were offered for the top five qualifiers over a three-month sales period. The top achievers would qualify for an incentive travel event in Hong Kong and the runners-up would go to Amsterdam for a long weekend with an oriental touch. To give the campaign some visibility at sales floor level sales assistants could win instant awards when the AEG local representative called, provided they could answer some basic questions about AEG products.

The results were impressive. Many of the major retailers increased their purchases by over 20% and some by as much as 50%, simply to ensure they would qualify for the trip to Hong Kong. From a business point of view the campaign provided a new channel of communication to their most important buyers and resources were concentrated on those with the capacity to buy more, rather than have efforts diluted by trying to appeal to the entire distribution network.

KEY INSIGHTS

The main value of the AEG scheme was the realization that by concentrating on those most likely to produce a profitable increase in business, they could be more effective in their use of resources. By targeting their resources on the top 25% they were able to offer a better chance of qualifying to their major retailers and be more efficient in terms of marketing activity. Also, by offering incentives to those who work on the sales floor they created a synergy in which both retail owner and employed sales representatives were focused on the same goals and not working to different agendas.

RETAIL (SNCF)

Sales at the sharp end are also about satisfying the customer so that they will return to use the service again in the future. SNCF, the French national rail services provider, needed to update its rather antiquated ticketing system and ensure that its ticketing agents with direct customer interface could use the new system confidently, enabling the organization to sell more services as part of the process. 7000 staff were involved throughout the entire country.

After extensive analysis of the communication and training issues involved it was decided that team-based training would be supported with an individual incentive based on actual performance targets using the new ticketing system. Personal performance would be monitored with 30% of performance credits to be given for knowledge of the new system and 70% reserved for actual on the job performance and sales. A proportion of credits was given for producing increased sales on routes where the normal buying pattern was known.

To get the main features of the new system across to all the customer-facing staff, nine training modules were developed in a comic strip format treating such topics as starting a conversation, talking to customers while the sale was being processed, deciding the best ticket option and offering appropriate discounts.

The credits accumulated by the retail staff could be redeemed by means of a combined merchandise and vouchers award catalogue. A hundred specific items of merchandise were sourced for those with limited access to retail outlets that could be ordered direct. Sales volume on a like-for-like basis increased significantly but of more lasting importance was the considerable improvement in technical fluency with the new system and the rise in levels of customer satisfaction which were monitored both before and after the introduction of the new processes.

The SNCF scheme is a good example of using sales rewards and incentives to support an administration task that at first sight is not an obvious candidate for incentives. Managements could argue that employees should undertake such tasks anyway and do not need rewarding specifically. However, it was clear at the early stages that SNCF wanted to avoid any potential dip in its levels of customer service and sales, even though it had to install new systems. In overall terms the rewards on offer were relatively modest in comparison to the development costs and the potential loss of revenue if staff were not fully behind the changes.

KEY INSIGHTS

The SNCF case highlights the need to think about incentives in conjunction with learning new skills or new product information.

It should never be assumed that salespeople relish the opportunity to receive more training. In fact, in many sales organizations training is often perceived as lost selling time and it is often difficult to get the commitment you need for managers in the field to have their staff trained properly in order to sell more. It's a question of one step backwards to take two steps forward. An incentive clearly helps to get commitment to learning new skills.

DISTRESS SERVICES (AUTOGLASS)

Autoglass is Europe's leading car-window replacement company. Customers call a telephone number when they experience a damaged windscreen or any related window problem. The call center relays the details to a field service of technicians who go to the customer whether they are at home or on the road to repair or replace the damaged window. The key dynamics of the business are therefore excellent service at the roadside and accurate information about the customer's situation.

Historically the organization had been paying out quarterly cash bonuses to all staff based on achievement of corporate profit targets. Unfortunately few staff in the work process could equate their everyday work performance to their quarterly bonus so few knew how to improve what they did to achieve a higher bonus. To make the payments more transparent Autoglass embarked on a performance-improvement program for all staff. After considerable analysis of job types they were able to categorize staff into four key areas: distribution, call handling, head-office and local branches. Each type of job was then broken down into key performance components to identify specific parts of the process which could be measured such as clerical errors, customer response times, repairs achieved and the correct picking of glass stock.

A standard was set for just three or four key activities that could be easily measured on a regular basis and performance was monitored on a monthly basis. Instead of cash, employees received retail vouchers of their choice from a wide selection. Because so many vouchers were being ordered the sponsors were able to command a considerable discount that helped to pay for the administration of the program. Staff received vouchers quarterly, based on their individual performance against the agreed standards for their peer group rather than for overall corporate performance.

Measurable improvements included the following.

- Abandoned calls (calls where customers hang-up without getting an answer) fell from 3.5% down to less than 1%.
- The average number of clerical errors in customer documentation fell from 20% to just 5%.
- Customer complaints fell from 12.5% to 7.5%.

The new program was clearly more visible to the staff than the previous cash bonus scheme as it highlighted specific behavior that required change. Because the rewards were easier to promote than cash they made a higher impact at the end of each quarter than cash that tends to get lost in the paycheck, along with all the other payroll items. On a wider note, the revised scheme enabled the organization to move from a customer-reactive business to one in which customer service was the driving force for change and strategic growth.

KEY INSIGHTS

This campaign shows the value of a proper re-appraisal of the incentive approach and the advantages of a willingness to change things around in a big way. Autoglass not only changed the reward itself but also changed the measurements used to such an extent that individuals felt personally responsible for their own improvement. If you can get individuals focused on their own contribution to the business within their sphere of influence then the organization as a whole will benefit.

FINANCIAL SERVICES (HONORS CLUB)

Although honors clubs in the American financial services sector have been around for many years the rest of the sales world has been relatively slow to apply this sales reward technique. The UK has probably been the quickest to apply the principles but as with all incentive planning it has to be appropriate to the local culture.

A major UK life assurance company with a large and well-distributed sales force was increasingly concerned about both its average sales per salesperson and its retention rates. They were not only selling less per individual but they were losing more employees just as they were about to become profitable. Each local area had to cover the costs of recruitment and basic training from their own budgets so the financial squeeze was on to get something done about it. The idea of an honors club was born.

It was decided that a new elite club of salespeople should be formed which would be aimed at the top 30% of the existing sales force. Within this top echelon there would be three levels; bronze, silver and gold. The proportions would be 15%, 10% and 5% respectively. Qualification would be on an annual basis and salespeople would have to re-qualify each year based on the current year's sales, but this could include repeat commission from existing clients too.

The rewards for qualification would be a mix of incentive travel, weekend breaks and recognition items. The Gold Club would fly long haul to an exotic location with their significant others, hosted by the company for a five-night event. Silver Club members would fly short haul with their partners and spend a long weekend at a top class leisure hotel, preferably with a golf course. Bronze Club members would be invited to a one-day sales convention packed with motivational speakers from their own industry and enjoy a gala dinner and cabaret. Qualifying members would receive a certificate and corporate jewelry appropriate to their level of qualification so that they could be recognized by their peers and by those back at their local branch office. The qualifiers' names would be featured in the sales magazine at the year end and their progress against re-qualifying would be published each month as each level would require a specific level of sales.

Average sales from the top 30% improved dramatically following the introduction of the new honors club and in aggregate proved to be enough for the organization to lose about one third of the poorer performers and their inherent costs of employment. Retention amongst the top 30% improved by some 10% thereby providing considerable training cost reductions. The honors club has now been in existence ten years and still provides the main communication channel of influence for its top producers.

KEY INSIGHTS

Large sales forces require specific incentive ideas to retain the interest and commitment of top performers, especially in the life assurance industry where sales skills are more highly prized than technical knowledge. By segmenting the sales force into manageable groups specific performance and incentive messages can be distributed to maximize the potential sales. Sales clubs follow the much-researched findings of Maslow's Hierarchy of Needs (see Chapter 2) where, beyond basic subsistence and survival, people can be motivated by a sense of belonging to a special group. Above this is the need to be recognized as having a specific skill, in this case that of an excellent salesperson.

CONSUMER ELECTRONICS (PHILIPS)

Travel sits at the very top end of sales incentives and rewards so incentive travel, where a group of high achievers is hosted by the organization on a lavish overseas event, is a major industry in itself. Philips Consumer Electronics sells brown goods through retail and wholesale channels but has to compete strongly for market share and consumer visibility. In the past they had used cash incentives and merchandise to reward major retail groups for their purchases but their market share had remained static. Prompted by their subsidiary in Hong Kong they decided to offer an invitation to top-performing purchasers to join them in Hong Kong and Borneo for seven nights. The event included island-hopping, a visit to an orang-utan sanctuary, white water rafting, tai chi lessons and even a visit to an orphanage in Borneo for charitable purposes. The campaign was themed A Walk on the Wildside, and destination-specific teasers were sent out regularly during the qualifying period.

Their market share rose from 5.3% to 9.5% as a direct result of the incentive travel incentive and sales rose an astonishing 76%.

KEY INSIGHTS

When money is no problem incentive travel can deliver spectacular results. However, it can work out to be a very expensive option. As partners are often included, there will probably be pressure to gross up the value of the award so that the sponsor can pay the tax on behalf of the recipient. Costs during the event are usually paid by the sponsor too. Because of the costs relatively few participants can enjoy the benefits so the skill is in presenting the program as if everyone can qualify, otherwise you may be accused of setting up a jolly for the chosen few with the consequent withdrawal of participation by the lower-achieving levels of the sales force.

MOST LIKELY USERS OF TRAVEL

Sales rewards and incentives presented as annual programs rely on relatively high-ticket products and healthy volumes. It is no surprise to discover therefore that there are certain types of organization that regularly use such techniques and others which do not, as a rule. In the 1990s some research was undertaken by the organizers of EIBTM (European Incentive, Business Travel and Meetings), an annual European exhibition that takes place in Geneva to bring together buyers and sellers in the incentives market. ITME in Chicago is a similar concept that services the American market. Part of the research was to rank the biggest users of incentive travel by market sector (and therefore incentives in general) across Europe. Table 7.1 shows the results.

As you can see from this list, financial services, automotive, and pharmaceuticals dominate as the main users of incentives, which fits in with the idea that it is the higher margin sectors which tend to use the more glamorous types of sales incentive. The usage can change depending on market conditions. IT for example took some heavy knocks in 2000 and after, which resulted in a considerable rethink on whether they could afford such overt expenditure in a weak market. This analysis should not preclude other market sectors from at least trying out various techniques but regular use is unlikely unless sales incentives become a strategic part of your offering to the sales force. In industry sectors where the sales skills required are truly transferable

Table 7.1 Who buys incentive travel? (Source: European Incentive Travel Survey/Touche Ross.)

Client sector	%
Pharmaceutical	10
Financial services	10
Automotive (units)	10
Automotive (parts)	9
Computing	9
Toiletries/cosmetics	9
Electronics	8
Electrical appliances	7
Office equipment	6
Farm equipment	5
Retail	5
Building materials	5
Heating/air conditioning	4
Leisure/catering	2
Other	1

often the incentive program becomes a large part of the seller's reason to stay loyal to one organization and as such should not be dismissed lightly or in a period of cost cutting. They can be highly effective retention devices.

CYCLICAL NATURE OF SALES INCENTIVES

Another phenomenon regarding the usage of incentives is that they tend to follow the general business cycle pretty closely. When economies are growing, high value incentives come to the fore as corporations chase conquest sales and the usage of incentive travel is very high, even by relatively small organizations. As the economy cools off, organizations generate fewer profits so cash and retail vouchers appear as the more likely type of incentive reward. The mechanics of incentive programs changes too. In the good times incentives are usually based on increased sales or sales with new customers. In a downturn incentives are more usually directed towards the maintenance of effective business processes and better back-office systems as there are so few sales to monitor. Often in these circumstances sales force incentives become "hygiene" schemes which aim to keep the channels of communication open with potential buyers so that when the market does start to pick up the sales force is in a good position to pick up the reins again. In such periods incentives could be based on activity such as courtesy visits or keeping up to date records rather than based on actual sales.

HUMAN AUDIT RESEARCH

Specific research into one organization's use of sales incentives is known as a human audit. Regular users of incentives are the most likely organizations to conduct a human audit as their returns on the expenditure may well be diminishing as the years go by. Or they may just need to take some views from the participants as to whether the program is still delivering. It can be a very profitable exercise, even by those organizations that are considered to be professional users. For example, Chevron Chemicals had introduced some five years previously an incentive program to reward good ideas. They wanted to know why it was not delivering the volume and quality of ideas that it used to generate in the early years. They discovered that 50% of the participants thought that their managers had too much say in who was given awards. Under the rules of the incentive scheme nominations were put forward to a management committee each quarter who then decided who was to receive what. It proved to be slow and cumbersome and unnecessarily bureaucratic.

The program was overhauled as a result of the human audit and the management committee aspect of the administration was abolished. The new program, Bringing Out The Best, included staff being empowered to recognize good practice whenever they encountered it in the working environment by completing a single sheet of paper and handing the bottom third to the nominated employee who could then use it to redeem a range of instant awards. To maintain the quality of the program each staff member was only allowed to nominate six incidents a year but there was no limit on the number of nominations any individual could receive.

Participation in the ideas incentive rose to 79% overall and 90% considered the revised scheme to be very good or excellent. The new feature whereby participants could recognize and reward good performance instantly was perceived by the participants to be the most beneficial amendment to the program.

Within the sales environment human audits have been used to clarify a number of issues that all too often are left unchanged, perhaps because the management feel threatened by criticism of their long-running scheme, which they have been involved with from the beginning. Typical issues include:

- choice of travel destination for the top achievers,
- choice of the secondary incentive rewards;
- lack of general participation;
- few newcomers seem interested;
- changes to the rules for qualification;
- communication issues;
- accuracy of figures on bulletins;
- redeeming low level rewards;
- target-setting;
- team versus individual credits; and
- formal recognition of success.

All these issues and more can be investigated using the human audit method. This can provide the opportunity for sales management to design a scheme to meet all the possible objections so that the program will be almost guaranteed a good reception when the details are finally made known.

LEARNING FROM EXPERIENCE

No two organizations are the same and this is as true of their experience of incentives as it is of any other shared corporate experience. Case histories are useful in that they show what is best practice and they sometimes point to what not to do. But there is no substitute for personal experimentation. If you have only ever run cash schemes before, you could start off with retail vouchers and compare the difference in performance. If you have a new intranet which your organization is using for internal communication, try commandeering the software developers to see if a sales incentive section of the site could be created to help you report on incentives more quickly than using paper and the mail. Use data manipulation techniques to analyze exactly what happens to your sales figures when you introduce incentives and make adjustments accordingly.

It may be that you need to consider a strategic program, which runs across all your sales activities throughout the year, overlaid with short-term tactical schemes for specific products or certain sales regions. After years of running incentives for your sales teams perhaps the key to synergy is the inclusion of the administration staff who support the sellers. This usually costs very little but the impact on overall performance can be disproportionately large. Or you may just feel that you are not getting the returns you expected but cannot put your finger on what is wrong. Using a human audit will give you all the answers.

Perhaps the final point to make is that markets and personnel change. They are in constant flux. Some gurus say that organizations change fundamentally as often as every two years. It makes sense therefore to mix up the incentive bag a little every so often to keep participants guessing and to be less predictable. The returns from incentives often far outweigh the investment required but you need the courage to keep the case for using sales incentives fresh in everyone's minds to avoid them being seen as an expensive luxury. If managed correctly they should always produce incremental profit.

12.07.08

Key Concepts and Thinkers

» Glossary
» Key concepts and thinkers

"I am Master of this college, what I don't know isn't knowledge."
Rev H .C. Beeching, Master of Balliol, Oxford, 1859-1919

GLOSSARY

Annual program - This is a general term to describe all the recognition and reward activities undertaken by the organization for a specific group of people. The program normally runs for twelve months and may include end of year rewards as well as short-term tactical promotions (see below). Some sponsors would include a conference or convention as part of the annual program even though the delegates may not need to qualify to attend.

Catalogue - The earliest incentive schemes in the US were built around merchandise catalogues so "catalogue" has been used as the generic term for the presentation medium for the rewards. In many cases it is still a printed brochure of the rewards on offer but it can also mean a promotional flyer or even an online presentation of items to be claimed for good performance.

Close-ended - If the participants in a program have to compete for a fixed number of rewards such as the top 10 or the top 100 highest performers, this is known as a close-ended scheme. The advantages to the sponsors are that they can budget exactly for the prizes to be awarded. However, they are less motivational and in general less effective than open-ended structures (see below). They are normally chosen by new users of incentive techniques or those without the financial resources to cope with the cash-flow implications of over-achievement.

Club concept - Otherwise known as honors clubs a club concept encapsulates the recognition aspects of any motivation or incentive program and could include corporate regalia, certificates, trophies or business support items which are awarded in addition to the incentive items. They are particularly prevalent within financial services and automotive organizations where good role models for the lower level participants are always welcome.

Designer awards - Such awards are a relatively new concept in which participants are encouraged to think up their own ideal rewards and the sponsor attempts to arrange the administration of them, provided the participant has achieved the relevant goal. For example, the ideal reward for a new home owner may be to have the house decorated by professionals or a film fan may want to meet a Hollywood star. By their nature such rewards may be difficult to organize and therefore expensive but they can add a highly personal dimension to any program which provides the higher achievers with something unusual and specific to aim for.

Escalators - Escalating is a target-setting structure in which participants have to stretch themselves more and more the higher they achieve. Typically a three-stage escalator could pay out rewards based on achievement of 100%, 110% and 125% of target with each higher level being a bigger stretch than the one before. This helps participants to push themselves to their personal limit when competing against a personal target.

Fast-start - One of the biggest challenges when launching an incentive program is to get noticed quickly by the participants who may have a number of equally important organizational messages to take on board. A fast-start normally means enhancing the credit given for any early sales so as to encourage participants to get involved at an early stage. Double credits for the first month of the campaign is a standard format. Its poor relation is the "fast-finish" in which enhanced credit may be given for the closing stages of an incentive scheme. This is a less successful idea as it normally means the organizer has set the target too high and needs to artificially create more winners than would be the case in better-planned circumstances.

Frequent buyer program - This is the term for a reward program for distributors, normally based on volume purchases, in which the more you order, the higher the rewards. The highest achieving participant may be invited on a hosted incentive travel event (see below) with their peers as a special reward. It is an incentive to increase purchasing. They are often run in conjunction with a sell-out program as no distributor necessarily wants to maintain high stocks indefinitely, so selling on the goods to customers is as important as buying them in.

Human audit - For full details see Chapter 6. The human audit is a research project that examines the motivational issues within a work group. In particular the human audit would survey attitudes and working practice regarding such matters as communication, skills development, reward choices and management style. It can be a very useful way to create incentive and reward programs that have built-in appeal to the participants before they are launched, since part of a good audit is to test incentive ideas to get a measure of their likely acceptance if implemented.

Incentive travel – One definition published by the UK Association of Incentive Travel Agencies goes as follows: "Incentive travel is that discipline of sales and marketing management which uses promise, fulfillment and memory of an exceptional travel related experience to motivate participating individuals to attain exceptional levels of achievement in their places of work or education." The travel event itself is usually an exotic, five-star destination with an organized ground program of sight-seeing and local dining, all organized by the sponsor.

Leaguing system – Participants in large, national programs are usually very diverse, with varying turnover and operating within different niches on behalf of a manufacturer or retail chain owners. They rarely face the same business issues on a day-to-day basis. For that reason it makes sense to group similar types of participant together to compete against each other on a like-for-like basis. They could be grouped by sales volume or type of product or number of staff or by geographic region, for example. Sometimes you may want to skew the winning places available in favor of your largest distributors to reward them for their support while still retaining a competitive element throughout the network. So, you could create leagues of different sizes, say leagues of five for the top volume people and leagues of twenty for the lower volume people, with two winning invitations to an incentive travel event for the top two in each league.

Leverage – All sales incentive and reward programs are in essence marketing tools to get the best possible sales performance for the least amount of investment. Discussions about leverage often take place during the planning stages of a program when the big question is what level of return can be expected by structuring the campaign in a particular way. This is known as leverage and needs to be quantified so that budgets can be set and objectives can be established. What leverage or incremental profit the planned program will create should be the major issue to be resolved before going ahead to the implementation stage.

Non-cash incentive - To distinguish merchandise, retail vouchers, travel, sports event tickets and the like from remuneration items such as salary, healthcare, pensions, bonuses and commissions the term non-cash incentive can be useful. It means any incentive or reward that is not money.

Open-ended - An open-ended incentive scheme is one in which participants compete against a target without reference to other participants. Such schemes are much more effective as motivational tools as participants are competing against themselves and their own target for rewards. They are particularly useful within a sales team with a wide distribution who may not meet very often and would therefore not be in competition with other employees on an everyday basis. The one disadvantage is that it is difficult to be precise about the eventual cost of the rewards as nobody can predict exactly who will achieve what. But in most well run organizations predictions of success are usually accurate enough for over-achievement not to become an internal cost issue, especially if each additional sale produces an incremental profit.

Performance improvement This is a general term for any kind of incentive program, whether for sales people or for support staff, which aims to create higher profits for the organization. Within the sales environment performance improvement is usually a measure of extra sales but it could equally be better adherence to administration processes or higher levels of prospecting, for example. Performance improvement agencies or consultancies are sales promotion specialists with a wide range of experience in helping clients set up and run incentive and reward schemes. They often have a marketing background but may well have their roots historically in the provision of certain types of reward such as group travel or merchandise.

Proposal - The proposal is what you may receive from a performance improvement or incentive agency as a result of information that you, the sponsor, give them about your current situation. It will include an outline structure, some creative, promotional ideas and an itemized costing of all the elements. If you aim to ask an outside firm to run your sales incentive program on your behalf you should ask at least two organizations to propose ideas as you can then compare the offerings from each one and form a judgment.

Standards program - Many manufacturers and owners of a business concept reward their wholesale and retail distributors on the basis of their compliance with set standards of business processes. This may cover how the products are presented in retail outlets, how well the salespeople are trained, levels of customer satisfaction and participation in advertising and promotional initiatives. Credits are given for levels of compliance and both cash and non-cash rewards are offered on the basis of performance against the criteria set down in the standards program. Automotive dealership networks are major users of standards programs but all retail premises could benefit from such schemes to ensure common levels of service and brand presentation.

Tactical campaigns - Not everything can be planned a year in advance in business. For that reason most annual programs (see above) include one or more tactical programs which offer incentives for short-term or product specific achievements. Typically a spring campaign or a mid-year scheme is introduced to complement the annual program and is often highly specific to meet a certain business need. Even though it may well be themed differently from the annual program it carries the same overall objective: higher sales.

KEY CONCEPTS AND THINKERS

Sales motivation is not an exact science. The principles on which many incentive programs are based can be found in any summary of human motivation and would include reference to Herzberg, Maslow and Mayo. (See *Motivation* by Philip Whiteley published in this series by Capstone, as part of the PEOPLE module, 09.07). You may also want to look up Victor Vroom, *Work and Motivation*, 1964[1] and McClelland, *Human Motivation*, 1984[2]. However, most academic research was not done with its application to business or organizations in mind. For that reason, it may be more useful to consider some of the key concepts in the context of the commercial arena and see how they might be applied in practice.

Goal setting

In Martin Ford's *Motivating Humans*[3] he outlined the three main factors that motivate human beings as goals, emotions and beliefs. Within a business context setting goals or objectives is a standard element of effective incentive programs. However, it is not just a question of getting your sums right. Clearly the rewards need to bear a relationship to the performance required otherwise you may end up paying too much for the improved performance. The objectives need to be measurable and fair.

Often sales programs are devised with far too many objectives, often conflicting, which leave the participants confused about what the sponsor wants them to do. In practical terms no more than three objectives should be put forward to participants, otherwise focus is lost and management are perceived as not really knowing what they want their teams to achieve. Typically there may be two sales measures and one quality measure, if only to curb ruthless selling at the expense of all-round customer service. The highest performers would therefore be those who are more rounded and are able to improve their performance on several levels, not just the one which involves clinching the deal. We all know the problems of going for short-term gains at the expense of long-term losses.

The second element in the area of goal setting for sales campaigns is for them to be perceived as fair. Equity theory emerged in the field of work motivation in the 1960s (Adams, Walster et al) as a major breakthrough in the understanding of levels of participation in organizationally inspired behavior programs. The principle goes back to Jung and Freud who realized that most of human motivation stems from a trade-off between pleasure and pain. If you set the barrier too high, participants will simply withdraw their co-operation and not compete at all, leading some management teams to then categorize all incentive programs as ineffective. On the other hand, if the task is too easy, not only will the sponsor lose money, participants may feel guilty about obtaining benefits too easily and disparage the scheme to others. So, when setting objectives you need to strike a balance or create equity in which the pain of the effort to achieve the goal is rewarded by the pleasure of an adequate and appropriate reward or compensation.

Throughout the 1980s and 1990s much theoretical work has been done in the area of classifying goal-directed behavior, this area having been largely neglected since the initial pronouncements of Maslow in 1943 about the hierarchy of needs. Goal-directed behavior has now been classified into a number of different areas, including affective, cognitive, subjective, social, safety and task-oriented. From a sales management point of view, the important fact to recognize is that humans are rarely one-dimensional and will respond to a range of messages at different times within their goal-directed behavior profile. Humans are complex creatures and rarely as mechanical as some psychologists would have us believe.

Reward selection and the middle-band concept

Those who are new to sales incentive planning often mistake the choice of reward as being the first crucial factor to decide. Most professionally organized sales incentives make the reward choice the last element to consider. Objectives, communications and adequate skills should be considered long before discussions about reward choice. However, choosing rewards can be problematical.

A number of surveys have revealed that the order of five reward types in terms of participant appeal is as follows:

1 individual or group travel
2 retail vouchers
3 merchandise
4 weekend breaks
5 sports event tickets.

Although this may be generally true it is not always true of every participant database. Young factory women and middle-aged doctors will undoubtedly have different mindsets when it comes to perceptions of an attractive reward. You may also need to consider the image of the sponsor and whether the reward choice matches the reputation of the organization. For example, most people would agree that a hosted incentive travel experience to an exotic location is an exciting reward but should a government department or a drugs provider be offering such rewards simply to get a commercial result?

You may also need to consider the lifestyle of the potential winners. Five nights at a top class hotel with gourmet dining may well be the best that money can buy but will your automotive showroom salespeople, for example, feel comfortable in such surroundings, especially if they have to buy their own drinks?

The cost of rewards also plays a part. Travel per head is expensive. Retail vouchers are relatively inexpensive. Often it is wise to create a series of different types of reward so that you can cater for all levels of the participant database. In most mature sales organizations people usually know who is at the top and who is at the bottom and a scheme which offers rewards at all levels merely reflects this reality. The best strategy is to try and spend most of the budget on the middle band of potential winners while leaving a smaller amount for the top end but make the top end rewards spectacular. Offering a trip to Rome for the top few will certainly help to get the program noticed but the majority of average performers would accept that they would need to produce exceptional performance to qualify.

Feedback theory, Ford & Lerner, 1992

Whenever serious research is undertaken regarding the factors for success or failure in sales incentive programs, communication always comes out as a vital issue. This should not be a surprise as social psychologists have been mapping how feedback on performance works since the 1970s. As Ford and Lerner put it in 1992: "When a process and its consequences are continually amplified by the effects of their own activity, the essence of positive feedback is present."[4] Individuals do not make progress towards goals without some kind of feedback as to how they are doing. In terms of sales incentives this means providing regular updates on achievements, both good and not so good, so that participants can adjust their behavior accordingly. An earlier study shows that focusing attention on "controllable short-term goals" is a major motivational strategy for any human activity (Barden & Ford, 1990[5]).

But feedback does not need to be formal, although a regular pattern of information helps. It could be a face-to-face briefing, a telephone call, e-mails or a letter through the mail. With high-flying salespeople often a personal call from someone way above them in the organizational hierarchy could be very effective when perhaps printed or report-format communications have become mundane and expected.

Motivation systems theory (MST)

This item was mentioned in Chapter 3 (Evolution of Sales Rewards and Incentives) but it does stand up as probably the most useful research work produced to date in the quest for understanding motivation within a business context. The principles outlined are all highly relevant to the world of targets, budgets and sales and when considered separately offer some keen insights into what may work and what will not work. However the key issue is to use all of the principles over time in an experimental way to get the best effect. Your record-keeping will need to be accurate and unbiased if you are to discover what works for your organization but the Equifinality Principle, as Ford puts it, is probably the most important. In other words, in life as well as in business there is rarely only one answer or one goal. Human beings are simply too complex. What we should look for is a number of ways to reach the ultimate goal and keep trying them out.

Sales incentives and rewards, unlike many other business issues, can be highly subjective. What works for one group will not necessarily work for another group. Human beings, especially those who act in teams, are highly variable and unpredictable. There are strong inter-personal dynamics at work as well as the added complication of an ever-changing economic and social environment. If people were totally predictable there would be no need to seek advice about the right sales incentive program for your team. The only certainty is that the more you try things out, the more you learn and the fewer mistakes you make. With experience you can minimize the risks of doing the wrong thing and losing the commitment and enthusiasm of your people who, in general, are genetically programmed to do their best, even if sometimes it does not come across that they are.

NOTES

1 Victor H. Vroom, (1964) *Work and Motivation*, John Wiley, New York.
2 D McClelland, (1985) *Human Motivation*, Scott, Foresman, Glenview, Illinois.
3 Martin E. Ford, (1992) *Motivating Humans*, Sage Publications, California.
4 Ford & Lerner, (1992) *Developmental systems theory: An integrative approach*, Sage Publications, Newbury Park, CA.
5 Barden & Ford, (1991) *Optimal performance in education*, Minneapolis, MN, Optimal Performance Systems.

Resources

» Useful organizations and consultancies
» Exhibitions and seminars
» Books, journals and references
» Networks and contacts

"I ran into Isosceles. He has a great idea for a new triangle."

Woody Allen

USEFUL ORGANIZATIONS AND CONSULTANCIES

BI Performance Services (USA)

A leading US performance improvement consultancy with early roots in merchandise programs, now with a recently acquired European subsidiary. www.biperformance.com

Grass Roots Group (Europe)

One of the largest UK agencies with a sound knowledge of process improvement techniques and an extensive European network of business partners.www.grg.com

Incentive Central.org

US-based promotional portal for the leading US consultancies and a useful gateway to other incentive-related Websites.

Incentive Marketing Association

The IMA is based in the US and includes suppliers from all the disciplines of incentive services except travel. It runs educational seminars at most of the major US trade shows and exhibitions.
www.incentivemarketing.org

International Society for Performance Improvement

The ISPI is a training-centered organization with over 10,000 members who come from both agencies and corporations and who have an interest in staff performance improvement. www.ispi.org

Incentive Travel & Meetings Association

London-based association of UK consultancies and European local support agencies offering access to a wide range of Europe-wide links for incentive planners. www.itma-online.org

Maritz (Worldwide)

The largest performance improvement agency in the world, based in St Louis, USA, with strong subsidiaries/joint ventures both in Europe and Asia. www.maritz.com

Performance Improvement Council (USA)

This is a loose association of the leading US performance improvement consultancies that come together to share best practice and act as a sounding board for industry-related issues. Contact is through Incentive Central (see above). www.incentivecentral/performance.org

p&mm (UK)

A leading UK agency with specific skills in web-based incentive and reward programs.
www.p-mm.co.uk

SITE (Worldwide)

The Society of Incentive Travel Executives has been operating for thirty years as an international, educational networking club of business events organizers, mostly involving incentive travel. It has over 20,000 members in more than 80 countries. www.site-intl.org

Saratoga Institute

A world-leading research organization that specializes in developing tools to measure performance at work. www.saratogainstitute.com

World Federation of Personnel Management Associations

A global federation of personnel management and human resources associations which represents over 300,000 members with a vast library of case histories available via the network. www.wfpma.com

EXHIBITIONS AND SEMINARS

Asia Pacific Incentives and Meetings Exhibition, Melbourne

Run by Reed exhibitions, this is the premier networking event for buyers and suppliers within the Pacific Rim who are looking for incentive travel services within the region.
www.aime.co.au

CIPD Convention, Harrogate

Annual event for UK human resources professionals held in the north of England with an extensive seminar program and good networking opportunities. www.cipd.co.uk

EIBTM, Geneva

The European Incentives, Business Travel & Meetings exhibition takes place in May each year in Geneva, Switzerland and attracts over 3000 exhibitors who are looking to sell into the European market. An awards evening was introduced recently to recognize excellence in the creation and planning of business events around Europe, some of which include the commercial use of incentive travel to achieve a business objective. www.travel.reedexpo.com

IMEX, Frankfurt

This is a new venture run by the former creators of EIBTM (see above) and due to take place in April/May each year in Frankfurt from 2003 onwards. It promises to offer 1500 exhibitors with over 2000 hosted buyers. www.imex-frankfurt.com

SITE University seminars, various locations

SITE (see above) as an educational foundation runs a number of SITE Regional Universities each year on aspects of incentive event management. www.site-intl.org

The Motivation Show (IT&ME), Chicago

Held each year in Chicago, usually in September, this is the leading industry showcase for agencies and reward suppliers who service the corporate incentives and performance improvement market. www.motivationshow.com

JOURNALS, BOOKS AND REFERENCES

Journals

Incentive (USA), monthly
Meetings & Incentive Travel (UK), ten times a year
Motivation Strategies (USA), eight times a year
Sales and Marketing Management (USA), monthly

Books

John G. Fisher, (2000) *How to Run Successful Incentive Schemes* second edition, Kogan Page, London

Bruce Bolger & Rodger Stotz, *Strategic Incentive Program Design* available from www.incentivemarketing.org

Victor H. Vroom, (1964) *Work and Motivation*, John Wiley, New York

Martin E. Ford, (1992) *Motivating Humans*, Sage Publications, California

Frederick Herzberg, (1959) *The Motivation to Work*, John Wiley, New York

Abraham Maslow, (1970) *Motivation and Personality*, Harper & Row, New York

David McClelland, (1961), *The Achieving Society*, Van Nostrand, New Jersey

Bernard Wiener, (1980) *Human motivation*, Holt, Rinehart & Winston, New York

Michael Armstrong, (2000) *Reward Management*, Kogan Page, London

John B. Miner, (1993) *Role Motivation Theories*, Routledge, New York

Over 50 case studies from various market sectors, part of the Incentive Promotions Campaign, including Pacific Bell Wireless, Honda, Cisco, Compaq, John Deere, IBM and many other market sectors can be found on the Incentive Marketing Website. www.incentivemarketing.org

NETWORKS AND CONTACTS

The world of sales incentives is a relatively small one in terms of obtaining practical and informed advice. Unless you have the time and the inclination to trawl through academic books, journals and reports on incentives in general the quickest way to get up to speed is to use your networking skills. The most instructive research is more likely to be done with current practitioners of sales incentives who probably work within fairly well-defined industry sectors such as automotive, pharmaceutical, financial, IT and retail. Over 85% of all incentive programs are managed on behalf of sponsors by the sales or marketing department, so start there. Most non-competitive sponsors are only too happy to give you an hour or so to go through their latest program and tell you how it is going.

Other sources include the annual awards ceremonies of various marketing journals that have a bias towards incentives. Often case histories of the winning programs will be written up in booklet form with details such as the number of participants, degree of sales improvement and illustrations of the promotional material. Many of these award winners will probably have submitted a much longer and more detailed case history than the one reprinted in the brochure so it is always worth making contact to see if you can meet up and discuss it.

Another more obvious source is other salespeople whom you know socially, perhaps from outside your own business sector. They probably participate in several schemes and will be highly informative about what works and what does not. Although you should be careful not to generalize from a single conversation they often have key insights about how to improve their current program. Your industry association may be able to put you in touch with specific sales managers who are known to be involved in incentive programs on a regular basis.

Finally, what about your clients and customers? Depending on your particular niche it may be possible to ask their advice about how to set up and run an effective incentive, especially if your customer is likely to become one of the participants. There is no substitute for asking the target audience about what they want. That's what marketing is all about, after all.

Ten Steps to Making Sales Rewards and Incentives Work

» Research the participants
» Agree your objectives
» Decide on a structure
» Check you can measure performance
» Create effective communication
» Select appropriate rewards
» Monitor the take-up
» Deliver the interim awards efficiently
» Publish the results
» Do post-campaign research

> "A mediocre (sales incentive) design which is well communicated, managed and administered is preferable to a technically excellent scheme which few people understand."
>
> *Michael Armstrong, author and remuneration specialist*

No amount of pre-reading and research can beat the learning experience of actually setting up and running your own scheme with your own people. It will be rewarding both personally and corporately but it can also be heart-breaking if it does not produce the results you intended. So, here are ten steps to help you make the right decisions for your team in your quest to produce the perfect sales incentives and rewards scheme.

1. RESEARCH THE PARTICIPANTS

Creating an effective sales incentive program is a marketing discipline and as such requires a good understanding of the potential target audience. In advertising this is achieved by researching the target market and trying out the proposition on a representative sample. Incentive planning is no different. The first task is therefore to conduct a human audit of some or all of your participants to see what would be acceptable and well received. If you have 500 or more participants, a sample of say 20% will be sufficient to get the answers you need. You should also look at past campaigns run within your organization and talk to some of the old-timers to get their views on what has been successful in years gone by.

The main issues to research are the structure of the organization (who manages whom, to do what), the numbers involved at each level, methods of communication and current performance standards or targets. There may also be a number of "soft" targets such as sales prospecting or presentation skills, which could be part of an activity-based incentive, rather than just basing everything on confirmed sales. Finally you may wish to float a few ideas to your sample in terms of the attractiveness of various types of reward to see what level of response you get. Once you have a clear idea of how your sales team operates and what is likely to work you can begin the creative process.

2. AGREE YOUR OBJECTIVES

Every incentive program needs clear and measurable objectives. Decide what uplift in performance you need to make the whole exercise worthwhile and start to do your figures. In broad terms a campaign target of more than 10% is usually enough both to pay for the scheme and create incremental profits for the organization. A stretch target of say 15%–20% is more challenging but if you are running an incentive for the first time, do not be surprised if it is much higher. Be careful not to base your profits on the most popular, lowest margin product. You need to consider whether adding extra credits for those lines which sell less well may be a good way to increase your turnover on difficult to shift products and so boost your profits.

As well as sales objectives it is always useful to include activity measures as activity almost always leads to sales in the long run. Add credits for prospecting, creating conquest sales, attending skills development courses, developing customer relationships or selling finance, if appropriate. The more you can reward the activity that leads to sales, the more likely sales will improve.

Take care that your objectives for the campaign do not run counter to other organizational goals or the impact of the program will be diluted. For example, running a scheme to sell a new product to your customer base should not normally include selling old stock at the same time or asking customers to complete some kind of administrative task. You need to be sure that the team goes into the field with a mission which is clear and uncomplicated, if the program is going to reach its full potential.

3. DECIDE ON A STRUCTURE

Although you clearly want to incentivize the best performers over the campaign period, handing out rewards to the same old faces will not generate the level of involvement you need to make the program profitable. Awards for the top 10 revenue generators in a sales team of 300 is not going to have the same impact as a program based on exceeding a personal target or qualifying in a niche category such as "best newcomer." You need a structure that will deliver the perception that everyone can win something, whatever base they are starting from.

The first thing to consider is how to direct most of the budget to the middle-band of achievers as, in total, the revenue generated from the middle 40% of the sales team will create the most opportunity for extra sales. One way could be to offer specific rewards (probably merchandise or retail vouchers) for exceeding their individual targets for the campaign period. If there are a lot of participants in your middle-band you may consider creating performance leagues so that similar level achievers compete with others at the same level.

For those who generally perform below par, you could create a one-off reward for achieving a basic level of performance as an encouragement. For those at the top end, a hosted travel or activity event for those who perform best nationally, would help to keep the high fliers competing once they have reached their personal target. By approaching the structure in this way you will have something promotional to say to most members of the sales team throughout the campaign and the collective improvement will be enhanced.

4. CHECK YOU CAN MEASURE PERFORMANCE

Although most organizations these days are awash with data and information, relatively few have the information stored in a way that helps you to monitor incentive performance. Sales figures are clearly the exception but what about prospecting activity, contact with existing clients, niche product sales by client or the number of presentations made or telephone calls made? Once you have decided what elements you wish to measure to arrive at an overall view of sales performance you may need some input from the IT department to create some software routines so that accessing the data on a weekly or monthly basis is trouble-free. Incentive schemes live or die by the speed with which information is mirrored back to the participants, so being confident that your figures are both correct and timely is of paramount importance.

Gathering information is costly. In some circumstances you may have access to a dozen or more categories of performance data but do you really need them all? In general you should aim to measure no more than three or four performance criteria to decide which participants are doing better than the others. If one of those criteria is proving difficult to capture it would be better to drop it and choose another rather than struggle on with a potentially flawed measure which the participants do not trust.

5. CREATE EFFECTIVE COMMUNICATION

Post-program research tells us constantly that of all the elements which could be handled better in incentive schemes, communication is the most important, but the one done the least well. It is not enough to offer the carrot of a sales incentive; you need to communicate the offer repeatedly and to all the different groups in the participant database to get the best returns. "Launch-it-and-leave-it" is the usual criticism coming from participants.

To begin with there should be an intriguing or uplifting theme rather than just Sales Program, 2003. It is often better if this theme is relevant to the overall objectives or strategy of the business such as "Quest for Quality" or "Better than the Best." This theme should then be used like an advertising slogan or brand whenever any communication goes out. The launch should be as exciting as the budget allows but should include an endorsement from local line management and a detailed briefing session so that any objections or misunderstandings can be discussed and hopefully dismissed.

Ongoing communication should include at the very least regular updates on performance, personalized to each participant. If there is a travel element in the rewards structure you could include teasers from the destination, hotel brochures, maps and anything else that may help get the message across that it is a trip worth qualifying for. At the end of the campaign it is always worth sending a wrap-up communication which states who won what and the relevant performances achieved. This not only helps to recognize superior achievement but also provides a stimulus, for those who did not quite make it, to up their game for the following campaign, especially if they know it will receive a similar level of publicity.

6. SELECT APPROPRIATE REWARDS

The general rule is that the rewards should suit the aspirational lifestyle of the participants, certainly at the middle and lower ends of the participant spectrum. It is tempting to set up rewards that cost a lot of money and let the value do the motivating but such items are rarely a good use of the budget. A trip on Concorde and five nights at a five-star hotel are certainly attractive but would be intimidating and possibly de-motivating for workers in a manufacturing plant who may never have been overseas before. Equally a portable TV or a microwave oven would be pointless for an insurance executive who already owns his or her own house in town and a condo on the beach.

In essence you need to consider how to offer each participant what they really want, which is impossible, so a compromise is inevitable. Merchandise catalogues have done this job for years allowing participants to choose what they want from a specific selection - but beware. Not all catalogues are the same and it is possible to specify to some catalogue suppliers the range of goods which are to be included and their values so that it contains items the participants would both want and aspire towards. The Internet is making such catalogues easier to produce. Now participants can themselves select the items online without having to wait for a printed brochure. Another popular alternative to the problem of giving people what they want is to offer retail vouchers so they can go and buy the items locally. A relatively new way to offer the widest possible choice is "designer awards" in which the reward administrators acquire the goods or service for the participant. This type of reward ranges from tickets to a specific sporting event to having the backyard landscaped or even violin lessons. There is a lot of creative fun to be had with such rewards but they do take time to organize and as such are usually only offered to the higher-level performers.

7. MONITOR THE TAKE-UP

If you have analyzed past sales patterns correctly you will be aware of the level of uplift you might get from the offer of a sales incentive. However, you should not wait until the end of the program to see how things are going. Performance averages, region by region, can be sampled to see what the uptake has been. It may be that a local manager is on holiday and may not have had the chance to brief the team with all the details. Or you may be recruiting a new management team. This would explain why some sales teams are not performing as well as you expected. Sometimes the reason for non-participation may be as simple as the fact that the brochures got lost in the mail or the system was down. More seriously, it could be that the performance targets were set too high and the participants have responded by not taking part at all. Investment in the set up of an incentive can be costly and none of it will be recovered unless you get good participation, so it is worth mothering the program in the early stages just to ensure that nothing untoward is going on.

One simple way to get a feel for how things are going is to do an e-mail or telephone survey in the first month both to check that the promotional items have been received and to verify that the participants understand what they have to do to qualify. In some technical sectors such as IT or pharmaceutical it is not unusual for first-month research to reveal that the rules are not clear as to how to win and so participation is less than expected. A quick e-mail to clarify the situation is often all that is needed to boost participation levels.

8. DELIVER THE INTERIM REWARDS EFFICIENTLY

The quickest way to lose the trust of your sales audience is to fail to do what you said you would do. Delivering on a promise is, after all, what selling is all about. Part of your reward plan may be to offer mid-campaign incentives for achievement over the first month or first half of the program. It is vitally important for the credibility of the campaign that these rewards are distributed in a timely fashion and according to the rules of the program. A "fast-start" reward which does not arrive until after the program has ended does little to endear the whole process to the winners and may well send a message to the non-winners that the scheme is not worth getting involved with if the promised rewards do not turn up.

Another reason for taking extra care with interim rewards is the fact that their distribution provides the sponsor with a promotional opportunity to take the campaign right into the heart of local sales areas through having them presented in the sales office or promoted in organizational magazines or Websites. Such action adds credibility to the program and will encourage lower level participants to up their performance over the second half of the campaign.

9. PUBLISH THE RESULTS

As soon as the program is over participants will be keen to see how well they have done. They will have a fair idea as you will have kept them up to date with regular performance updates but the closing weeks of any campaign are usually very busy with last minute sales and so it is natural to want to know how many of them made it into the reckoning. One of the issues will be that some costly rewards at the top end will be distributed on the basis of total program performance so all the claims have to be properly checked and verified. This takes time and may involve discussions with technical personnel and senior managers to make sure that all the claims are bona fide. It is a good idea to send a holding memo to the participants to let them know that the campaign clean-up process will take longer than the normal end of month data check so they should not expect confirmation of the final results for say two to three weeks, or whatever is appropriate.

It goes without saying that any travel event being planned for the top achievers should not be scheduled too close to the end of the campaign period for the same reason. Three months is a good time-lag as often winners need to give good notice to other family members if they are going to be away from home for more than a few days, not to mention the possibility of having to acquire a visa or have inoculations.

10. DO POST-CAMPAIGN RESEARCH

If you have opted to do a human audit before you start your campaign it makes sense to apply the same technique once the program is over. Post-campaign research allows you to check on whether what you planned to happen actually did happen and will highlight any improvements you need to make for next time. One of the most important advantages of an audit is finding out what participants thought of the rewards on offer and the mechanism by which they received them. Often a simple change of administration can substantially enhance the next program.

The other advantage is that the comments will help you to create the next program with informed feedback rather than just guessing what might work well. The final aspect is to do a cost/benefit analysis of cost incurred against extra revenue generated so that when the hullabaloo of the program has been forgotten there is something on record to show that it was a net generator of revenue rather than just another sales cost.

KEY LEARNING POINTS

- There is no substitute for experience so however well your program goes it is always worth listening carefully to the users' experience of the campaign to adjust things for next time.
- Markets and economic conditions change constantly. What was a good scheme the previous year may not be appropriate 12 months later so before you roll out last year's program take a sense check on what is going on in the outside world before simply changing the numbers.
- Communication is most likely the element of your campaign which could be done better so be very critical about how the program is presented and, if there is time, ask some potential participants to give you their views before you commit yourself to a national roll-out.
- The Internet is throwing up new communication options on a regular basis, especially regarding the redemption of rewards. Keep your options open about any new software available to make the process of delivering the rewards as painless as possible.
- A sound business rationale is vital if good sales incentive programs are to be repeated, as many organizations only see the cost of such schemes in their financial reviews. Having a case history to hand which shows the incremental gain from the previous program can only strengthen the case for doing the next one.

Frequently Asked Questions (FAQs)

Q1: What's the best incentive for salespeople?

A: The choice of reward depends on the profile and lifestyle of the participants. See Chapter 6 for more details of how organizations match rewards to the participants.

Q2: Why not just increase commission to improve sales performance?

A: Beyond the comfort zone salespeople respond to non-cash more effectively than cash. See Chapter 2 for why cash produces diminishing returns and Chapter 3 for the motivational theory behind sales rewards and incentives.

Q3: Do incentives really work in today's more sophisticated business environment?

A: There are many examples of specific bottom-line improvements as a result of using targeted incentive programs. Chapter 7 outlines a number of successful schemes including Volvo, AEG and Philips.

Q4: What are the key things I need to know about putting a program together?

A: Chapter 8 runs through the main concepts you need to consider before you commit your organization to an incentive initiative.

Q5: Is there anything specific I should know if I want to run my domestic program overseas?

A: This is a very complex area as it is more about local culture and values than choice of reward or campaign structure. See Chapter 5 for a discussion about the likely global issues.

Q6: Has the Internet made any difference in how I should organize an incentive scheme?

A: It certainly has and quite dramatically. See Chapter 4 for full details of the recent e-dimension to sales incentive planning.

Q7: How do I find out more about the subject?

A: Chapter 9 runs through the main sources of up-to-date information regarding sales reward and incentive programs.

Q8: Where do I start when it comes to planning a program for my team?

A: See Chapter 10 for a step-by-step guide.

Q9: What element of the plan is the most important?

A: Research tells us that communication is always the most critical issue for success. See Chapter 6 for the options you need to consider.

Q10: Should I run the program myself or ask an agency or consultancy?

A: It will depend on the size of the scheme in terms of administration and the critical need to get it right. See Chapter 9 (Resources) to help you decide.

Acknowledgments

I am mostly grateful to all the clients I have worked with over the past 20 years to help me form a view about what constitutes best practice when it comes to creating effective sales reward and incentive programs.

More specifically, I am indebted to John Sylvester, p&mm, the UK incentive specialists, for access to the IBM case history and to Larry Schoenecker at BI Inc (USA) for Mazda Cars and many other interesting business performance improvement ideas.

Index

EXPRESSEXEC – BUSINESS THINKING AT YOUR FINGERTIPS

ExpressExec is a 12-module resource with 10 titles in each module. Combined they form a complete resource of current business practice. Each title enables the reader to quickly understand the key concepts and models driving management thinking today.

Innovation

01.01 *Innovation Express*
01.02 *Global Innovation*
01.03 *E-Innovation*
01.04 *Creativity*
01.05 *Technology Leaders*
01.06 *Intellectual Capital*
01.07 *The Innovative Individual*
01.08 *Taking Ideas to Market*
01.09 *Creating an Innovative Culture*
01.10 *Managing Intellectual Property*

Enterprise

02.01 *Enterprise Express*
02.02 *Going Global*
02.03 *E-Business*
02.04 *Corporate Venturing*
02.05 *Angel Capital*
02.06 *Managing Growth*
02.07 *Exit Strategies*
02.08 *The Entrepreneurial Individual*
02.09 *Business Planning*
02.10 *Creating the Entrepreneurial Organization*

Strategy

03.01 *Strategy Express*
03.02 *Global Strategy*
03.03 *E-Strategy*
03.04 *The Vision Thing*
03.05 *Strategies for Hypergrowth*
03.06 *Complexity and Paradox*
03.07 *The New Corporate Strategy*
03.08 *Balanced Scorecard*
03.09 *Competitive Intelligence*
03.10 *Future Proofing*

Marketing

04.01 *Marketing Express*
04.02 *Global Marketing*
04.03 *E-Marketing*
04.04 *Customer Relationship Management*
04.05 *Reputation Management*
04.06 *Sales Promotion*
04.07 *Channel Management*
04.08 *Branding*
04.09 *Market Research*
04.10 *Sales Management*

Finance

05.01 *Finance Express*
05.02 *Global Finance*
05.03 *E-Finance*
05.04 *Investment Appraisal*
05.05 *Understanding Accounts*
05.06 *Shareholder Value*
05.07 *Valuation*
05.08 *Strategic Cash Flow Management*
05.09 *Mergers and Acquisitions*
05.10 *Risk Management*

Operations and Technology

06.01 *Operations and Technology Express*
06.02 *Operating Globally*
06.03 *E-Processes*
06.04 *Supply Chain Management*
06.05 *Crisis Management*
06.06 *Project Management*
06.07 *Managing Quality*
06.08 *Managing Technology*
06.09 *Measurement and Internal Audit*
06.10 *Making Partnerships Work*

Organizations

07.01 *Organizations Express*
07.02 *Global Organizations*
07.03 *Virtual and Networked Organizations*
07.04 *Culture*
07.05 *Knowledge Management*
07.06 *Organizational Change*
07.07 *Organizational Models*
07.08 *Value-led Organizations*
07.09 *The Learning Organization*
07.10 *Organizational Behavior*

Leadership

08.01 *Leadership Express*
08.02 *Global Leadership*
08.03 *E-Leaders*
08.04 *Leadership Styles*
08.05 *Negotiating*
08.06 *Leading Change*
08.07 *Decision Making*
08.08 *Communication*
08.09 *Coaching and Mentoring*
08.10 *Empowerment*

People

09.01 *People Express*
09.02 *Global HR*
09.03 *E-People*
09.04 *Recruiting and Retaining People*
09.05 *Teamworking*
09.06 *Managing Diversity*
09.07 *Motivation*
09.08 *Managing the Flexible Workforce*
09.09 *Performance and Reward Management*
09.10 *Training and Development*

Available from:
www.expressexec.com

Life and Work

10.01 *Life and Work Express*
10.02 *Working Globally*
10.03 *Career Management*
10.04 *Travel*
10.05 *Flexible and Virtual Working*
10.06 *Lifelong Learning*
10.07 *Body Care*
10.08 *Free Agency*
10.09 *Time Management*
10.10 *Stress Management*

Training and Development

11.01 *Training and Development Express*
11.02 *Global Training and Development*
11.03 *E-Training and Development*
11.04 *Boardroom Education*
11.05 *Management Development*
11.06 *Developing Teams*
11.07 *Managing Talent*
11.08 *Developing and Implementing a Training and Development Strategy*
11.09 *Developing the Individual*
11.10 *Managing Training and Development Finance*

Sales

12.01 *Sales Express*
12.02 *Global Sales*
12.03 *E-Sales*
12.04 *Complex Sales*
12.05 *Account Management*
12.06 *Selling Services*
12.07 *Sales Rewards and Incentives*
12.08 *FMCG Selling*
12.09 *Customer Relationships*
12.10 *Self Development for Sales People*

Customer Service Department
John Wiley & Sons Ltd
Southern Cross Trading Estate
1 Oldlands Way, Bognor Regis
West Sussex, PO22 9SA
Tel: +44(0)1243 843 294
Fax: +44(0)1243 843 303
Email: cs-books@wiley.co.uk

9 781841 124605